NOSH
GLUTEN-FREE
by Joy May *& the family team*

@NOSHBOOKS

D1080566

NEW

NOSH SUGAR-FREE GLUTEN-FREE
JOY MAY
ISBN: 9780993260919

NOSH GLUTEN-FREE BAKING
JOY MAY
ISBN: 9780956746498

NOSH GLUTEN-FREE
JOY MAY
ISBN: 9780956746450

NOSH QUICK & EASY
JOY MAY
ISBN: 9780956746481

NOSH FOR STUDENTS
A FUN STUDENT COOKBOOK
5TH EDITION
OVER 300,000 STUDENT NOSH BOOKS SOLD
JOY MAY
ISBN 9780993260933

NOSH FOR STUDENTS VOL.2
JOY MAY
ISBN: 9780956746467

VEGETARIAN NOSH FOR STUDENTS
A FUN STUDENT COOKBOOK
OVER 3,000,000 STUDENT NOSH BOOKS SOLD
JOY MAY
ISBN 9780993260940

NOSH FOR BUSY MUMS & DADS
JOY MAY
ISBN: 9780956746443

Contents

letter from Joy...

I first started writing this book for the numerous people who had requested a book on gluten-free eating and also for a number of friends who are gluten intolerant. I was always looking for recipes to help them, or, in the case of my friends, to feed them. During the cooking and writing process, I stopped eating wheat and found that the stomach pains, with which I had been struggling for years, ceased almost immediately. I realised that I, too, am gluten intolerant!

Since this great enlightenment, I have been on a 'journey' discovering new ingredients and, far from just making do with gluten-free living, I have been really enjoying it. The avoidance of stomach pains aside, I have loved the lightness of cakes and cookies without gluten and just the extra variation of ingredients that can be used.

One of my biggest challenges was getting a bread recipe to work well. I am really happy with the three that I have included in this book (at one point I wasn't sure I would even get one recipe to work), but I think that extra bread recipes are going to be a lifelong pursuit from here on.

So, I am with you all on the voyage into the wonders of gluten-free living. Keep an eye on our web site "noshbooks.com" as we will be posting lots of yummy, gluten-free stuff.

Enjoy cooking,

Joy

P.S. I love to see how people are getting on with my recipes. Why not tweet a photo of your plate using "#noshbooks". I'll be watching out for it!

Why Gluten-Free?

The most common reason for people eating a 'gluten-free' diet is that they have either coeliac disease or just a general intolerance of wheat and gluten. Coeliac disease is an auto-immune disease affecting the gut and other parts of the body. Along with gluten intolerance, it commonly gives symptoms such as bloating, abdominal discomfort, muscular disturbances, headaches, migraines, severe fatigue and bone or joint pain. If we are gluten 'intolerant', when we eat gluten, it can cause the lining of our gut to become inflamed and therefore diminishes its ability to absorb certain nutrients. Before going on a completely gluten-free diet, it is recommended that you consult a doctor.

These days, many fitness instructors and sportspeople recommend a wheat and gluten-free diet. Wheat converts to sugar faster than any other grain, the sugar then converts to fat which is deposited on the hips, thighs and tummies. Many would also agree that wheat affects our gut's ability to absorb nutrients essential for a healthy body. People who have cut out all traces of modern wheat from their diet have found they have major improvements in health and physical performance. Novak Djokovic, for example, fundamentally relates his leap in success to a change in diet away from gluten products.

Our Approach

These might seem common sense to some, but I hope they help a little. In my efforts to get things right, I have binned many things, and have given up on some ideas. What you see here is the result of lots of testing but you don't see all the failures. I have thrown away so many loaves of bread in search of a good result. Hopefully, my failures will save you a lot of time. Just give things a try. Rather than just cutting out the ingredients that cause problems, I have sought new ones as replacements and enjoyed eating things I have not cooked with much before.

I have found, especially in savoury cooking, that you can just substitute the normal flour with gluten-free flour, normal pasta with gluten-free, etc, and the food is totally fine for the rest of the family. In fact, most of the time, they hardly notice. However, in baking, it is not always so simple. You often need to add a little more baking powder or something like 'xanthan gum'. The gluten in normal wheat flours is the ingredient that gives elasticity and bounce to bread or cakes and holds them together. Some will recommend lots of different kinds of flours, but, in this book I have, as a rule, used Doves Farm plain and self-raising flour. It usually contains a mix of rice, potato, tapioca, maize and buckwheat flour. Rice flour can also work well in things like Victoria Sandwich (see page 190). Remember to use gluten-free baking powder and bicarbonate of soda. I have tested all the recipes in this book many times to make them work well, so I hope you enjoy cooking and eating them.

I had hardly ever used polenta before writing this book and thought that it was just bland, but I have found it to be an excellent carrier of flavour. Even in itself it can be quite tasty. One example would be when making polenta chips, of which there are a couple of recipes in the book. Even when using the ready-made polenta and just adding seasoning, once the chips are browned, they taste great. Thankfully, this does not involve any deep frying. It is also great for making a creamy mash (see page 80). Polenta makes excellent cakes; they do have a different, crumbly texture (see page 194).

I find gluten-free pasta usually takes longer to cook than the normal stuff, but you need to be careful not to overcook, as it becomes very gluey, especially spaghetti. Adding a little olive oil to the pasta after cooking stops it sticking together. Quinoa is a grain which works really well in cold or warm salads. Our only problem with this ingredient is that Tim despairs when the rest of us find it impossible to pronounce the word!

I have now built up a good storecupboard of interesting gluten-free products which I find very helpful (see page 11).

I always make a weekly menu plan before shopping. This makes cooking a much less frustrating process.

So...what *can* I eat?

The safest way to cook is to make your food from fresh ingredients. It is best to avoid pre-cooked and pre-prepared foods, such as sauces, cook-in sauces, burgers, ready-meals, etc. Many things are subject to cross-contamination during production, so best to go for the things specifically labelled 'gluten-free'. Check the labels of anything you buy.

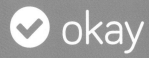 okay

Gluten-free foods	Gluten-free alternatives
✓ fresh fruit and vegetables	✓ rice flour
✓ fresh meat and fish	✓ buckwheat flour (despite the name, it is not related to wheat)
✓ fresh dairy products	
✓ fresh eggs	✓ almond flour
✓ spices and herbs	✓ tapioca flour
✓ plain peas, beans, lentils, pulses	✓ soy flour
✓ plain nuts and seeds	✓ potato flour
✓ plain white, brown and wild rice	✓ chickpea flour
✓ plain corn (maize, sweetcorn)	✓ coconut flour
✓ tofu and soya	✓ quinoa
✓ sugar and honey	✓ polenta (cornmeal)
✓ pure oils	✓ cornflour

Note: 'Plain' refers to no additives.

? think about it

Buy gluten-free versions

- oats
- stock cubes - Knorr, the most widely available brand, are GF
- corn tortillas and corn chips
- food sauces, marinades and even soy
- cakes and biscuits
- burgers and sausages
- baking powder
- bicarbonate of soda
- suet and vegetarian suet
- baked beans - sauce may contain wheat, but some Heinz are OK.

Traces of gluten*

- curry pastes
- mustards, chutneys and pickles
- mayonnaise
- some soft cheeses
- potato crisps - plain can be ok, but many flavoured ones contain traces of gluten
- sweets & chocolate
- ice creams and desserts
- dry roasted nuts
- gravy granules
- soya milk
- rice milk
- ready-made foods like frozen chips, waffles and instant mash

* You may be able to buy GF versions

❌ no way!

Grain based - AVOID

- wheat
- normal plain and self-raising flours
- couscous
- semolina
- spelt
- barley - found in beer, malt extract,
- malted milk and some vinegars
- rye
- bulgar wheat
- cereals

Contain gluten - AVOID

- coffee and tea whiteners
- flavoured yoghurt & fromage frais
- pre-prepared grated cheese

Where can I buy gluten-free ingredients?

Many of our everyday ingredients are readily available in the supermarkets as gluten-free versions. You may need to shop around between them. Opposite is a chart giving information about who stocks what, although, obviously, this can change with time. The bits and bobs are all there for you to buy online (see below), but I suggest that you buy your favourite ingredients in bulk, as the postage is sometimes a bit steep.

Online

	abelandcole.co.uk	healthysupplies.co.uk	mexgrocer.co.uk	hollandandbarrett.com	westcountryspice.com	spicesofindia.com	goodnessdirect.co.uk	amazon.co.uk
almond flour		✓	✓				✓	✓
corn tortillas and chips			✓					✓
curry paste	✓	✓				✓	✓	✓
hoisin sauce	✓			✓				
tamari soy sauce		✓	✓				✓	✓
multigrain quinoa pasta		✓						✓
oyster sauce								✓
range of curry pastes				✓	✓	✓	✓	✓
suet								
teriyaki sauce		✓					✓	✓
zero noodles				✓				✓
rice and buckwheat porridge		✓					✓	✓

NOTE: all of this data was correct on Jan 2016

Supermarkets

	ASDA	Waitrose	Sainsbury's	TESCO
baking powder	✓	✓	✓	✓
beer	✓		✓	✓
bread	✓	✓	✓	✓
biscuits	✓	✓	✓	✓
cakes	✓	✓	✓	✓
cereals	✓	✓	✓	✓
chickpea (gram) flour	✓		✓	✓
chorizo		✓		
ciabatta	✓	✓		✓
corn chips		✓		
cornflakes	✓	✓	✓	✓
flour: bread flour, brown and white	✓	✓	✓	✓
flour: buckwheat flour		✓	✓	
flour: plain and self-raising flour	✓	✓	✓	✓
flour: rice flour		✓	✓	✓
granola	✓	✓	✓	
mayo	✓			
meusli	✓	✓	✓	✓
muffins	✓	✓	✓	✓
naan bread			✓	✓
oats	✓	✓	✓	✓
pasta: general & spaghetti	✓	✓	✓	✓
pasta: lasagna sheets		✓		✓
pesto (Meridian and Sacla)	✓	✓	✓	✓
pitta bread	✓	✓	✓	✓
polenta (corn maize)	✓	✓	✓	✓
quinoa	✓	✓	✓	✓
ready-made polenta				✓
rice noodles	✓	✓	✓	✓
rice puffs		✓	✓	✓
sausages	✓	✓	✓	✓
stock pots	✓	✓	✓	✓
wild rice	✓	✓	✓	✓
xanthan gum	✓		✓	

Your Guide to Gluten-Free Pasta

SEASON SEASON SEASON

With gluten-free pasta, more than with normal pasta, don't forget to season well with salt while cooking.

WATER, WATER EVERYWHERE

Always cook the pasta in plenty of boiling water, especially spaghetti, as it can stick together quite easily.

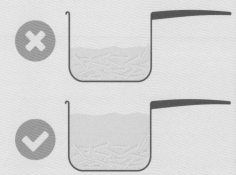

DON'T TRY TO BE A HERO

Don't cook too much pasta in one pan at a time. If you are cooking for a lot of people, you might want to try using two pans, instead of cramming it all into one.

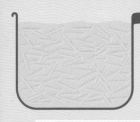

IT'S STICKY STUFF

Stir the pasta during the cooking process to make sure it doesn't stick together. When it is cooked and drained, add a tablespoon of olive oil and mix.

IGNORE THE PACKET

Keep testing it yourself. Gluten-free pasta generally needs a little longer to cook, but not necessarily as long as the packet states. It tends to go a bit 'gloopy' if cooked for too long.

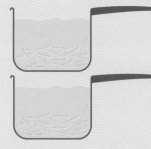

orecupboard

usly, your storecupboard is going to change. I would suggest that you build up the
ing gluten-free ingredients which feature in the book:

- polenta: fine polenta (cornmeal) and ready-made polenta
- GF plain and self-raising flour
- rice flour
- GF brown and white bread flour
- xanthan gum
- GF baking powder
- rice: basmati, Arborio and mixed rice
- GF corn tortillas
- different kinds of GF pasta
- GF spaghetti
- GF lasagna sheets
- GF oats
- quinoa: dried and ready-cooked
- GF stock cubes
- GF curry paste
- GF soy sauce
- GF hoisin sauce
- cornflour
- GF bread and breadcrumbs

What is quicker than just grabbing a mug and filling it. What is easier to remember as a unit of measure than a mug of this or 2 mugs of that!

This book is designed so that you don't need to use weighing scales, but we have included the gram/millilitre measures for those of you who prefer a bit more precision.

Throughout the book, I have used a mug to measure ingredients. This mug holds $^1/_2$ a pint or 300ml of liquid and is the exact size of the mug pictured opposite. So find a mug that measures up to this one and you won't go far wrong.

This actual mug is the same one I used when writing my first book back in 2000, it has a place in my heart. Although it is now cracked, it still has a special spot in our mug cupboard!

a mug =

ACTUAL SIZE

Snacks usually comprise sandwiches or something on toast, so there are one or two of those ideas here. We have also included some soups, salads, breakfasts and other odds and ends.

TESTER #1

Helen

I live in Reading with my husband Peter, our two children, Clare and Matthew, two cats, two rabbits and a plethora of fish. I'm a full-time mum.

I've been completely gluten-free since November 2011, when I was diagnosed Coeliac. It was completely out of the blue, as there's no family history of it at all. I suffered for about 15 years with various symptoms, but, when I eventually went to the doctor, I was diagnosed with IBS.

The 'Cantonese Lemon Chicken' is absolutely fantastic! I've waited nearly three years for Chinese food and it was worth the wait. The recipe was very straightforward and tasted delicious - it will definitely become a staple in our house.

Just like your Nosh for Busy Mums and Dads, I think this book will encourage me to cook more from scratch. Although I plan meals week-by-week, we tend to eat the same things, but the book has encouraged me to try new things and vary our menus a bit.

SNACKS

Smoked Mackerel Kedgeree

In my opinion, mackerel is one of the most underrated fish. It is widely available, ready-cooked and vacuum packed, in most supermarkets. This makes it extremely convenient to keep in the fridge.

1 ½ mugs **basmati rice**

2 mugs defrosted frozen **peas**

4 hard-boiled **eggs**

1 tablespoon **olive oil**

6 spring **onions**, chopped

2 tablespoons **GF Korma curry paste**

500g **smoked mackerel**

2 tablespoons freshly chopped **coriander**

1 Put the rice in 3 mugs boiling water and simmer for 12 minutes. Add the defrosted peas to the pan and leave, with the lid on, until needed.

2 Put the eggs on to simmer for 10 minutes. Drain off the water and leave them sitting in cold water (stops the dark lines forming around the yolk).

3 Heat the oil in a wok, add the onions and fry for 1 minute. Add the curry paste and cook for 30 seconds.

4 Take the skins off the mackerel and flake the fish. Add to the pan, along with the cooked rice and peas.

5 Serve with the coriander and chopped up, boiled eggs.

Avocado & Puy Lentil Salad with Tangy Lime Dressing

This salad has a lovely fresh feel, with some different flavours, together with some very healthy ingredients.

Lime Dressing

juice of 2 **limes**

2 tablespoons **olive oil**

1 teaspoon **sugar**

salt and **pepper**

bag of **mixed herb leaves**

400g tin **puy lentils**, drained and rinsed

250g **cherry tomatoes**, each cut in half

4 **spring onions**, chopped

1 **yellow pepper**, chopped

2 ripe **avocados**, peeled and cut into chunks

1 tablespoon freshly chopped **parsley**

1 tablespoon freshly chopped **coriander**

handful **pine nuts**

100g **feta cheese**, crumbled

1 Mix the dressing ingredients together.

2 Arrange the herb leaves on the plates.

3 Mix the salad ingredients together (apart from the feta) and divide between the 4 plates. Sprinkle the feta over the top.

4 Add the dressing.

Rosti with Frizzled Eggs & Ham

We sometimes now use rosti in place of toast since I started eating gluten-free and it is certainly no hardship for the family. Rosti makes a good breakfast or midday snack. The spinach and egg flavours here go really well together.

1 **onion**, grated

4 medium **potatoes**, grated

1 **sprig rosemary**, chopped finely

2 tablespoons **olive oil**

4 **eggs**

4 slices **ham**

100g bag **spinach**, roughly chopped

1 Mix together the onions and potato, squeezing out any excess liquid, season and mix in the rosemary.

2 Heat the oil in a large frying pan and divide the mixture into 4. Place the potato mix in the pan and flatten down each rosti. Cook on a medium heat for about 10 minutes, turning every now and then.

3 Remove from the pan. Add the eggs and fry on quite a high heat so that the eggs are frizzled and crispy around the edge. Take eggs out of the pan.

4 Add the spinach to the pan, it will take seconds to wilt in the hot pan.

5 Serve the rosti with the ham, spinach and eggs.

Flaked Trout with Dill & Potato Salad

Delicious light flakes of trout sit perfectly with the potato salad. The dill makes it just that bit more special. Great Saturday lunchtime meal.

750g **new potatoes**, cut into bite-sized pieces

small bunch **spring onions**, chopped

5 **pickled cucumbers**, chopped (**or gherkins**)

3 tablespoons **crème fraîche**

2 tablespoons **mayo**

juice of a **lemon**

2 tablespoons freshly chopped **dill**

1 tablespoon **olive oil**

4 **trout fillets**, approx 350g

bag **salad leaves**

Dressing

juice of a **lemon**

2 tablespoons **olive oil**

salt and **pepper**

1 teaspoon **sugar**

1 Add the potatoes to a pan of boiling water. Bring to the boil and then simmer for 10 minutes, or until the potatoes are tender. Drain and leave to one side.

2 Mix the spring onions, cucumbers, crème fraîche, mayo, lemon juice, and dill together in a large bowl and season. Add the cooked potatoes and mix well.

3 Heat the oil in a frying pan and gently fry the trout on both sides. It should take no more than five minutes to cook. Peel off the skin and flake the fish.

4 Meanwhile combine the dressing ingredients.

5 Serve the fish on top of the potato salad, together with the salad leaves. Drizzle the dressing over the salad leaves.

🌐 How does a warm, salmon salad sound? Go to: www.noshbooks.com/warm-salad

£0.52 /PERSON · SERVES 15 · EASE ★★☆☆☆ · PREP 10 MINS · COOK 30 MINS · V

Home-Made Muesli with Apricots & Cranberries

This makes an excellent alternative to a bought muesli. It is easy to make and you can vary the fruits as you wish. Great with some fruit and yoghurt for breakfast.

3 tablespoons **sunflower oil**

1 tablespoon **runny honey**

450g packet **rice and buckwheat porridge**

100g **coconut flakes**

100g **flaked almonds**

300g **ready-to-eat apricots**, chopped

100g **dried cranberries**, roughly chopped

1 Preheat the oven to 160°C fan oven/180°C/gas 4.

2 Mix the oil and honey together. Put the rice and buckwheat flakes in a large bowl and pour the oil mixture in. Mix together well with your hands.

3 Spread the flakes out onto a large baking tray and place in the oven for 10 minutes.

4 Add the coconut flakes and the almonds and mix together. Return to the oven for a further 10 minutes. Stir everything around and return to the oven for a final 10 minutes.

5 Add the fruits while the flakes are still warm and stir around.

6 Once cooled, transfer into an airtight container.

Leek & Stilton Soup

Although this is pretty traditional, you may not have tried Stilton in a soup.

50g **butter**, measure using the packet

2 **leeks**, sliced

4 medium **potatoes**, peeled and cut into 2cm chunks

4 mugs **boiling water**/1200ml + 2 **GF veg stock cubes**

200g **Stilton cheese**

2 tablespoons **double cream**

chives to garnish

GF bread to serve

1 Heat the butter in a large saucepan and add the leeks and potatoes. Fry until they begin to brown.

2 Add the water and stock cubes and bring to the boil. Turn down to simmer for 15 minutes.

3 Crumble the cheese into the soup. Add the cream and season well. Blitz with a hand-held blender until smooth. Serve with some bread and fresh chives.

🌐 Trust us, this 'Apple and Celery Soup' is a cracker too: www.noshbooks.com/apple-soup

Carrot & Apple Soup with Cashews

Vibrant in colour, vibrant in taste. The combination of the cooking apple and the cashews gives this soup a sweet and sour tang. It looks amazing. Great for a midweek meal or Saturday lunch.

50g **butter**, measure using packet

4 medium **carrots**, peeled and sliced

1 large **onion**, sliced

1 medium **potato**, cut into 2cm cubes

1 large **cooking apple**, peeled and sliced

4 mugs **boiling water**/1200ml +
2 **GF chicken or veg stock cubes**

50g **cashews**

2 tablespoons **olive oil**

3 slices **GF bread**.

1　Heat the butter in a large saucepan and add the vegetables and apple. Fry for 4–5 minutes.

2　Add the water, stock and cashews and bring to the boil. Turn down to simmer for 20 minutes.

3　Meanwhile, make the croutons. Heat the oil in a large frying pan and dip in the bread to make sure the oil is spread over the three slices. Fry on each side until browned. Remove from the pan and cut into croutons.

4　Blitz the soup with a hand-held blender and serve with the croutons.

Spinach Potato & Streaky Bacon Frittata

Frittatas are a quick and easy way to make a snack for 4 people in one pan.

200g **streaky bacon**

1 tablespoon **olive oil**

4 medium **potatoes**, cut into 2cm cubes

200g **baby leaf spinach**

8 **eggs**, beaten

1 mug grated **Parmesan cheese**

salad to serve

1 Fry or grill the bacon until it is crispy. Cut into bite-size pieces.

2 Heat the oil in a large frying pan and add the potatoes. Season well and fry on a medium heat for 10 minutes with a lid on the pan. Turn frequently to allow even browning.

3 Once the potatoes are cooked, add the chopped spinach, replace the lid and leave for 1–2 minutes for the spinach to wilt.

4 Preheat the grill.

5 Add the eggs and bacon to the pan and gently mix. Season well. As the egg sets on the bottom of the pan, gently move the mixture to allow runny egg to get to the bottom and the sides of the pan.

6 When the egg is almost set, sprinkle the Parmesan over the top and place the pan under the grill for about 5 minutes for the cheese to melt and brown a little.

7 Serve with some salad.

🌐 See another frittata recipe online:
www.noshbooks.com/fritatta

Chilli & Basil Beefburgers

If you don't have a food processor, just chop everything finely and mix together with your hands to make the burgers.

Burgers

1 **red onion**
1 clove **garlic**
1 **fat red chilli**
500g good **beef mince**
handful **basil**
1 tablespoon **olive oil**

Sauce

1 tablespoon **mayo**
1 tablespoon **yoghurt**
1 **pickled cucumber**, finely chopped

100g **streaky bacon**
4 **GF burger buns**
lettuce
tomatoes, sliced

1 Put the onion, garlic and chilli in a food processor and whizz until everything is finely chopped. Add the mince, basil and seasoning. Whizz together. Form into 4 burgers.

2 Heat a little oil in a large frying pan and fry the burgers on a medium heat for about 10 minutes each side.

3 Meanwhile, mix together the sauce ingredients.

4 Fry or grill the bacon until it is crisp.

5 Serve in the buns with the salad, bacon and the sauce.

🌐 Why not try this posh, blue cheese, stuffed burger:
www.noshbooks.com/blue-cheese-burger

BLT with Guacamole

Guacamole

1 ripe **avocado**

1 tablespoon **yoghurt**

1/2 **fat red chilli**, finely chopped

juice of half a **lemon**

salt and **pepper**

200g **bacon**

8 slices **GF bread**, we used the brown seeded bread on page 170

2 **little gem lettuces**

2 **tomatoes**, sliced

1 To make the guacamole, peel the avocado and mash with a fork. Mix in the rest of the ingredients.

2 Fry the bacon until crisp. Make up the sandwich with the guacamole on the bottom.

Olive Tapenade & Poached Egg on Soda Bread

Splendid Saturday breakfast fare. An easy way to poach eggs is in a frying pan. Fill almost to the brim with boiling water and then turn it down to simmer very gently. Break an egg into a mug and lower the mug below the surface of the water and allow the egg to gently drift out. You can do about 4 at once and allow them to cook quite slowly. Scoop out with a slotted spoon.

Olive Tapenade

2 mugs **green olives**

1 clove **garlic**

2 **anchovies**

3 tablespoons **olive oil**

1 tablespoon **capers**

4 **eggs**

4 slices **GF bread** (we have used soda bread here (see page 168)

1 Put the tapenade ingredients in a food processor, season and whizz for 30 seconds. Spread over the bread.

2 Poach the eggs and serve on top.

36 snacks

Spiced Quinoa with Ham & Feta

Quinoa is Spanish in origin and is grown for its edible seeds. It is related to the beetroot and spinach families of foods. It is high in protein and, happily, is gluten-free.

1 tablespoon **olive oil**

1 teaspoon **ground coriander**

1/2 teaspoon **cumin**

250g packet of **ready-to-eat, red and white quinoa**

50g **toasted flaked almonds**

4 **spring onions**, chopped

2 tablespoons freshly chopped **coriander**

120g sliced, **cooked ham**, chopped

juice of 1/2 **lemon**

bag **salad**

Dressing

juice of 1/2 **lemon**

2 tablespoons **olive oil**

salt and **pepper**

1 teaspoon **sugar**

150g **feta cheese**, crumbled

1 Heat the oil in a frying pan and fry the spices for 30 seconds. Add the quinoa and fry for 30 seconds.

2 Mix together the flaked almonds, spring onions, coriander and ham in a bowl. Add the quinoa to the bowl along with the lemon juice.

3 Divide the salad among the plates, sprinkle over the dressing. Serve the quinoa mix on top and then crumble over the feta.

Salami & Rocket Tortillas with Balsamic Dressing

Although these are specifically corn tortillas, they can contain traces of gluten if they are manufactured alongside other products. Be sure you can get gluten-free. They are available from www.glutenfree-foods.co.uk.

Balsamic Dressing

1 tablespoon **balsamic vinegar**

1 tablespoon **olive oil**

1 teaspoon **sugar**

salt and **pepper**

4 corn **GF tortillas**

4 dessertspoons **yoghurt**

6 **spring onions**, chopped

4 sliced **tomatoes**

150g sliced **salami** or **other spicy meat**

1 mug grated **Cheddar cheese**

1 bag **rocket leaves**

1 Preheat the grill.

2 Mix together the dressing ingredients.

3 Place the tortillas on the base of the grill pan. Spread a dessertspoon of yoghurt over each tortilla.

4 Divide the spring onions and the tomatoes between the tortillas and season. Twist the salami and slot in between the tomatoes and sprinkle the cheese over.

5 Put under the hot grill until the edges of the tortillas go brown and a bit crispy, and the cheese begins to bubble.

6 Serve with the salad on top and sprinkle over the dressing.

Mushroom Soup
with Onion & Pumpkin Seed Garnish

Tim (responsible for the photographs in the book) said, at first, he did not want me to make mushroom soup, as he said every mushroom soup in history has always looked like wallpaper paste. He 'graciously' conceded he was wrong! The garnish is well worth making.

Garnish

1 **red onion**, cut into 2mm rings

2 tablespoons **pumpkin seeds**

2 **mushrooms**, sliced

2 tablespoons **olive oil**

Soup

1 tablespoon **olive oil**

50g **butter**, measure using packet

1 **onion**, sliced

2 cloves **garlic**, chopped

300g **cup mushrooms**, sliced

200g **chestnut mushrooms**, sliced

3 mugs **water**

1 tablespoon **GF concentrated vegetable stock** or one **GF veg stock cube**

2 tablespoons **long grain rice**

3 sprigs **thyme**

1 mug/300ml **double cream**

1 Preheat the oven to 200°C fan oven/220°C/gas 7.

2 To make the garnish, place the onion rings, pumpkin seeds and sliced mushrooms on a large baking tray or roasting tin. Drizzle with olive oil and season. Mix together and then spread everything out on the tray. Place in the oven for about 20 minutes, or until everything has browned.

3 Meanwhile, make the soup. Heat the oil and butter in a large saucepan and fry the onions and garlic until the onions begin to soften.

4 Add the mushrooms and fry for 1 minute.

5 Add the water, stock, rice, and thyme and season well. Bring to the boil and then turn down to simmer for 15 minutes.

6 Remove the thyme and blitz with a hand-held blitzer. Add the cream.

7 Serve with a little of the garnish in each bowl.

Thai Chicken Salad with Flaked Almonds

2 tablespoons **toasted sesame oil**

3 **chicken breasts**, cut into bite-sized pieces

250g **chestnut mushrooms**, sliced

1 tablespoon **GF red Thai curry paste**

2 tablespoons **honey**

1 tablespoon **olive oil**

juice of a **lime**

3 tablespoons toasted **flaked almonds**

1 bag **salad leaves**

1 Heat the oil in a frying pan or wok. Add the chicken and fry until it is no longer pink.

2 Add the mushrooms and fry for 2-3 minutes. Remove from the pan.

3 Add the curry paste and cook for 30 seconds. Add the honey, olive oil, lime juice and almonds. Mix together and fry for 30 seconds.

4 Add the chicken and mushrooms back to the pan and mix everything together.

5 Serve with the salad leaves.

🌐 Here's another chicken salad recipe:
www.noshbooks.com/chicken-honey

Spicy Lamb Wraps with Minted Mushy Peas

You might be surprised to see mushy peas not within the four walls of a chip shop. I assure you, they are right at home with these spicy lamb wraps.

Lamb Patties

500g **minced lamb**

2 teaspoons **cumin**

1 teaspoon **paprika**

1 **fat red chilli**, finely chopped

1 tablespoon **olive oil** to fry

Mushy peas

4 mugs defrosted frozen **peas**

2 tablespoons freshly chopped **mint**

juice of 1/2 **lemon**

25g **butter**, measure using packet

Tzatziki

300ml **Greek yoghurt**

1/2 **cucumber**, grated and liquid squeezed out

juice of 1/2 **lemon**

salt and **pepper**

8 **GF corn tortilla wraps**

1 Mix together the pattie ingredients, season and form 8 patties. Heat the oil in a large frying pan and fry the patties on a medium heat for about 2 minutes each side. Check one to make sure it is cooked through.

2 Meanwhile, put the peas in boiling water and simmer for 2 minutes. Drain, add the mint, lemon, butter and some seasoning and mash.

3 Mix together the tzatziki ingredients.

4 Serve everything together in the wraps.

We all dash home at the end of the day and need to find something quick to eat. Here are lots of ideas that take between twenty and thirty minutes to prepare.

TESTER #2

Helen

I am a mother of 3 young children. Food is important to us as a family, so we work hard to provide healthy, home cooked food everyday. Both my husband and I run our own business so life is certainly full right now!

The 'Tortilla Layered Beef and Bean Pie': oh my goodness, a complete family winner! So simple to make and very tasty. Cannellini beans are lovely and flavoursome, surprisingly it's not a heavy meal either, just fulfilling.

I will definitely use this book for my family. As a whole, I think we all eat too much gluten and 'stodge', even when we do maintain a healthy lifestyle, as so much of it is hidden in our food nowadays. It makes me consider every ingredient we have in our food and therefore what we are giving our children.

Pan-Fried Cod Steak with Tomato & Olive Risotto

1 tablespoon **olive oil**

1 **red onion**, chopped

1 mug **Arborio rice**

2 mugs/600ml **water**

1 **GF fish stock cube**

250g **chestnut mushrooms**, sliced

250g **cherry tomatoes**

24 **black olives**, roughly chopped

1/2 mug grated **Parmesan cheese**

2 tablespoons freshly chopped **basil**

1 tablespoon **olive oil**

4 pieces **cod steak**

1 Heat the oil in a large frying pan or wok. Add the onion and fry until it begins to soften.

2 Add the rice to the pan and cook until the rice absorbs the oil. Add the water and stock cube.

3 Add the mushrooms and tomatoes and bring to the boil. Turn down to simmer, with a lid on the pan, for 15 minutes. Add the olives, Parmesan and basil and heat through for 30 seconds.

4 5 minutes before the end of the cooking time for the risotto, heat the other tablespoon of oil in a frying pan and fry the fish on a medium heat. Season well as it fries and cook until it is lightly browned on both sides and cooked through.

5 Serve together with the risotto.

Cajun Chicken & Quinoa Apricot Salad

You can buy ready-cooked quinoa. It is a very versatlie ingredient, full of protein and easy to use.

2 mugs/600ml **boiling water + 1 GF chicken stock cube**

1 mug/160g **quinoa**

100g **ready-to-eat dried apricots**

4 teaspoons **Cajun spice mix**

3 **chicken breasts**, thinly sliced

2 tablespoons **olive oil**

1 bunch **spring onions**, thinly sliced

3 tablespoons freshly chopped **coriander**

1/2 mug/50g **pine nuts**

yoghurt to serve

1 Put the quinoa in a saucepan with the water and chicken stock. Bring to the boil and then turn down to simmer for 18 minutes. Add the chopped apricots and simmer for another 5 minutes. The water should be absorbed. Set to one side until needed.

2 Put the Cajun spice on a plate and toss the chicken pieces in it.

3 Heat the oil in a large frying pan and then fry the chicken on a medium heat for 4–5 minutes until the chicken is cooked through.

4 Add the spring onions, coriander, pine nuts and quinoa to the pan, season well and mix together.

5 Serve with the yoghurt.

Quick & Easy Paella

You could use 100g of roughly chopped, fresh spinach, instead of the frozen, if you wish. I find the frozen stuff quite handy and a little cheaper.

2 tablespoons **olive oil**

1 **red pepper**, chopped

6 **spring onions**, chopped

2 cloves **garlic**, finely chopped

100g **diced chorizo**

2 **chicken breasts**, cut into bite-sized pieces

1 mug **risotto rice**

2 mugs **water**

1 tablespoon **GF chicken stock**

1 tablespoon **tomato purée**

300g **cooked prawns**

4 pieces frozen **spinach**, defrosted

2 tablespoons freshly chopped **coriander**

juice of a **lemon**

1　Heat the oil in a wok or large frying pan. Add the pepper, onions, garlic and chorizo. Fry until the chorizo begins to brown.

2　Add the chicken and fry until it is no longer pink.

3　Add the rice and fry until the rice has absorbed the liquid from the pan.

4　Add the water, stock and tomato purée, bring to the boil and then simmer for 10-12 minutes, or until the rice is tender.

5　Add the prawns and the spinach and cook for 2-3 minutes.

6　Add the coriander and the lemon juice, mix and serve.

Soufflé Ricotta Pancakes with Avocado Salsa & Tzatziki

We call these soufflé pancakes, because they are so light and fluffy on the inside!

Salsa

1 **avocado**, peeled and cut into small chunks

3 **tomatoes**, chopped

juice of 1/2 a **lemon**

1 tablespoon **olive oil**

Tzatziki

1/4 **cucumber**, grated and liquid squeezed out

2 **pickled gherkins**, chopped

3 tablespoons **yoghurt**

Pancakes

3 **eggs**

250g **ricotta**

1/3 mug/50g **GF self-raising flour**

25g melted **butter**

2 tablespoons freshly chopped **chives**

2 tablespoons freshly chopped **basil**

2 tablespoons **olive oil** to fry

bag of **rocket leaves**

1   Mix together the salsa ingredients and season well.

2   Mix the tzatziki ingredients together.

3   Separate the egg whites from the yolks, retaining both. Mix the egg yolks and the ricotta together. Add the flour and mix well.

4   Beat the egg whites until they are stiff. Gently fold into the yolk mixture, along with the herbs and melted butter, and season.

5   Heat some oil in a frying pan and add tablespoons of the mixture to the pan to make individual pancakes. Fry on a medium heat. Once the bottom of the pancake is browned, carefully flip over and cook the other side. The mixture will make about 10 pancakes.

6   Serve with the tzatziki on top of the pancake, the salsa next and some rocket leaves over the top.

Coconut Cod Kedgeree

Kedgeree, the old favourite with its Indian origins, is still a winner today. The coconut milk adds a new twist and gives a sweeter taste.

1 1/2 mugs **basmati rice**

400ml tin **coconut milk** + 2 mugs **water**

2 tablespoons **oil**

4 small pieces **cod**

1 **onion**, chopped

1 **red pepper**, chopped

3 tablespoons **GF Korma curry paste**

1 mug frozen **peas**, defrosted

1   Put the rice, coconut milk and water in a saucepan, bring to the boil and then turn down to simmer, with a lid on the pan, for 12 minutes. Set to one side until needed.

2   Meanwhile, heat 1 tablespoon of the oil in a large frying pan and add the fish. Season well and fry on a medium heat for 2 minutes each side. Remove from the pan and set to one side.

3   Add the other tablespoon of oil to the pan and fry the onion and pepper until the onion begins to soften. Add the curry paste and fry for 30 seconds.

4   Add the rice and the frozen peas to the pan and mix well. Flake the fish and add to the pan. Mix gently so as not to break up the fish completely.

5   Serve.

Chorizo Calabrese with Quinoa Pasta

Quinoa contains lots of protein. The pasta is available on the internet, see page 8. If you don't have time to get some, just replace with normal gluten-free pasta.

3 mugs **multigrain quinoa pasta**

1 **broccoli**

2 tablespoons **olive oil**

1 **onion**, sliced

250g **chorizo**, sliced

6 **tomatoes**, chopped

juice of a **lemon**

1 Put the pasta on to boil with the chopped stalks of the broccoli. Simmer for 3 minutes and then add the broccoli heads and simmer for another 4 minutes. Drain and return to the pan.

2 Meanwhile, heat the oil in a large frying pan or wok. Fry the onions until they begin to soften. Add the chorizo and fry until it begins to brown. Add the tomatoes and fry for 2 minutes. Season well and add the lemon juice.

3 Mix in the pasta and broccoli and serve immediately.

TESTER #3

Angie

I am originally from Brazil and have a grown-up family. I sampled some of Joy's GF meals and was especially amazed at the taste of the cakes. As a result, I started to eat less and less ingredients with gluten, and noticed that I was feeling much better regarding a bloating tummy and heartburn problem. Neither I nor my GP had made the crucial link to gluten causing the problem. I have now eaten gluten-free for 7 months and have not missed anything. In fact, the cakes and bread are delicious.

Pan Fried Potatoes with Chicken Spinach & Blue Cheese

Quite an unusual salad. Tasty, quick and easy to make and full of some excellent nutrition.

2 tablespoons **olive oil**

4 medium **potatoes**, cut into 2cm cubes

1 **red onion**, sliced

3 **chicken breasts**, cut into bite-sized pieces

250g **cherry tomatoes**

300g **spinach**, roughly chopped

150g **blue cheese**

1 Heat the oil in a large frying pan. Add the potatoes and fry on a medium heat for 10 minutes, with a lid on the pan. Turn frequently.

2 Add the onions, fry for a further 3 minutes and season.

3 Add the chicken and fry for a further 4 minutes, stirring frequently.

4 Add the tomatoes and fry for 1 minute.

5 Add the spinach and fry for 1 minute.

6 Crumble over the blue cheese and serve immediately.

Chicken & Mushroom Pilaf

If you like things more spicy, then you can add more curry paste, or even chop up a fat, red chilli and add with the peas at the end.

1 mug **basmati rice**

1 teaspoon **pilau rice seasoning**

2 tablespoons **olive oil**

1 **onion**, chopped

250g **mushrooms**, sliced

1 dessertspoon **GF rogan josh curry paste**

3 **chicken breasts**, cut into small bite-sized pieces

1 **GF chicken stock cube** + 1/4 mug **water**

1 mug frozen **peas**, defrosted

1 tablespoon freshly chopped **coriander**, optional

1   Put the rice in 2 mugs boiling water. Add the pilau rice seasoning and bring to the boil. Turn down to simmer for 12 minutes. The water should be fully absorbed.

2   Meanwhile, heat the oil in a large frying pan or wok and fry the onions until they begin to soften.

3   Add the mushrooms and fry for 2-3 minutes.

4   Add the curry paste and the chicken and fry until the meat is no longer pink. This should take 3-4 minutes.

5   Add the water and crumble in the stock cube. Add the peas and simmer for 5 minutes.

6   Add the cooked rice and coriander and mix together.

7   Finally mix in the fresh coriander and serve.

🌐 Here's a 'Chicken and Lentil Pilaf' to try as well:
www.noshbooks.com/lentil-pilaf

£ 1.63 /PERSON · SERVES 4 · EASE ★★☆☆☆ · PREP 10 MINS · COOK 35 MINS · OK TO FREEZE ❄ · V

Quinoa Salad with Red Pesto & Roasted Vegetables

Meridian is a brand of pesto which I have found is gluten-free and available in supermarkets.

2 **sweet potatoes**, peeled and cut into 1cm dice

2 **red peppers**, roughly chopped

1 **red onion**, sliced

1 **aubergine**, cut into 1cm dice

2 cloves **garlic**, chopped

4 **tomatoes**, cut into 2cm chunks

3 tablespoons **olive oil**

250g pack of **precooked red and white quinoa**

2 tablespoons **red pesto**

1 tablespoon **olive oil**

juice of a **lemon**

1/2 mug grated **Parmesan**

1 Preheat the oven to 200°C fan oven/220°C/ gas 7.

2 Put the vegetables on a large roasting tray. Season and drizzle over the 3 tablespoons of oil. Mix everything together and spread out evenly. Place in the oven for 35 minutes, or until things are nicely browned.

3 Take out of the oven and mix in the quinoa.

4 Mix together the red pesto, 1 tablespoon oil and the lemon juice. Stir into the veg mix.

5 Serve with the Parmesan sprinkled over the top.

Minted Lamb Meatballs with Balsamic Tomato Sauce

Gluten-free spaghetti needs to be cooked in a large pan with plenty of water. It only needs to be cooked for about 5 minutes, as opposed to the 9 specified on some packets. Just test it every now and then and don't allow it to overcook.

Meatballs

500g **minced lamb**

2 tablespoons freshly chopped **mint**

1 **egg** yolk

1 tablespoon **olive oil** to fry

Sauce

2 tablespoons **olive oil**

2 **red onions**, sliced

2 cloves **garlic**, finely chopped

500g **passata**

1 tablespoon **balsamic vinegar**

1 tablespoon **brown sugar**

2 tablespoons **sun-dried tomato paste**

1 **GF lamb stock cube**

GF spaghetti

1   Mix together the lamb, mint, egg yolk and season. Form into approx 16-18 balls.

2   Heat the oil in a large frying pan and fry the meatballs for about 10 minutes, turning them frequently so they brown on all sides.

3   Meanwhile, make the sauce. Heat the oil in a large saucepan or wok. Add the onions and fry until they begin to soften.

4   Add the rest of the ingredients, season and bring to the boil. Simmer for 5 minutes.

5   Meanwhile cook the spaghetti. Drain and stir into the sauce.

Ginger Mirin Chicken with Zero Noodles

We only discovered zero noodles whilst writing this book. They are made from a plant extract called 'glucomannan', are very low in calories and have a high fibre content.

Sauce

1 tablespoon **cornflour**

3 tablespoons **GF soy sauce**

2 tablespoons **mirin**

1 mug **water**

1 **GF chicken stock pot**

2 tablespoons **toasted sesame oil**

1 **red pepper**, chopped

bunch **spring onions**, chopped

120g **shiitake mushrooms**, sliced

3 **chicken breasts**, cut into bite-sized pieces

3 tablespoons freshly grated **ginger**

2 cloves **garlic**, finely chopped

100g **cashew nuts**

2 tablespoons freshly chopped **coriander**

400g **zero noodles**

1 Mix together the cornflour, soy, mirin, water and stock pot. Leave to one side until needed.

2 Heat the oil in a large frying pan or wok. Add the pepper and onions. Fry for 1 minute. Add the mushrooms and chicken and fry for a further 4 minutes.

3 Add the ginger and garlic and fry for 1 minute, then add the sauce mix. Bring to the boil and then turn down to simmer gently for 3-4 minutes. Make sure that all the chicken is cooked through. Season well.

4 Meanwhile, take the noodles out of the pack and rinse well under cold water. Put in a pan of boiling water. Simmer for 2 minutes and then drain.

5 Add the cashews and coriander and serve with the noodles.

£ 1.38 /PERSON

SERVES 4

EASE ★★☆☆☆

PREP 30 MINS

Pancetta & Sweet Potato Risotto

50g **butter**, measure using packet

200g **pancetta lardons**

1 bunch **spring onions**, chopped

4 large **tomatoes**, chopped

2 **sweet potatoes**, peeled and diced

1 mug **Arborio rice**

6 **mushrooms**, sliced

2 mugs **water**

1 **GF chicken stock cube**

3 tablespoons freshly chopped herbs: **basil**, **parsley** or **coriander**

1 Heat the butter in wok and fry the pancetta lardons until they begin to brown. Add the onions, tomatoes and sweet potatoes and fry for 2-3 minutes.

2 Add the rice to the pan and fry for 30 seconds, allowing it to absorb the butter. Add the mushrooms, water and stock cube, and season. Bring to the boil and then turn down to simmer, with a lid on the pan, for 12-15 minutes or until the rice is tender.

3 Stir in the herbs and serve.

🌐 For another super-simple risotto, go to:
www.noshbooks.com/simple-risotto

Thai Cod & Coconut Curry

Great blend of fish and coconut. Really easy to make and a great way to pack in some omega 3's.

1 ½ mugs **basmati rice**

2 tablespoons **sesame oil**

6 **spring onions**, chopped

1 **yellow pepper**, cut into small pieces

1 tablespoon freshly grated **ginger**

1 clove **garlic**, finely chopped

1 tablespoon **GF Thai red curry paste**

400ml can **coconut milk**

350g **white fish**, **cod** or **haddock**, cut into bite-sized pieces

1 tablespoon freshly chopped **coriander**

1 Cook the rice in 3 mugs of boiling water. Simmer with the lid on for 12 minutes. Set to one side until needed.

2 Heat the oil in a large frying pan or wok and fry the onions and pepper for 1 minute. Add the ginger and garlic for 30 seconds. Season with salt and pepper. Add the curry paste and fry for 30 seconds.

3 Add the coconut milk and the fish and bring to the boil. Turn down to simmer for 5 minutes. Sprinkle with the coriander.

4 Serve with the rice.

Chicken & Chestnut Mushroom Marengo

Chicken Marengo is named after the dish Napoleon ate after he won the battle of Marengo. He needed a quick meal and, apparently, all his chef, Dunard, had was garlic, chicken, tomatoes and herbs. Not sure when the pasta was added. However, it is quick to make and very tasty.

2 tablespoons **GF plain flour**

2 **chicken breasts**, cut into bite-size chunks

2 mugs **GF pasta**

3 tablespoons **olive oil**

1 **onion**, sliced

1 clove **garlic**, finely chopped

6 **tomatoes**, chopped

250g **chestnut mushrooms**, sliced

2 tablespoons **tomato purée**

1/2 mug/150ml **white wine** (or water) + 1 **GF chicken stock cube**

2 tablespoons freshly chopped **basil**

1   Put the flour on a plate and season well. Toss the chicken pieces in the flour until they are well coated.

2   Cook the pasta, drain and return to the pan.

3   Heat the oil in a large frying pan and fry the chicken until it is browned on all sides and cooked through, (check one of the larger pieces). Take out of the pan and set to one side.

4   Add the onions and garlic to the pan and fry until the onion begins to soften.

5   Add the tomatoes and mushrooms and fry for 1 minute. Then add the tomato purée, wine or water and chicken stock. Bring to the boil and simmer for 2 minutes.

6   Add the basil, check the seasoning and add more, as required.

7   Stir in the pasta and serve with the chicken on top.

£ 1.45 /PERSON · SERVES 4 · EASE ★★☆☆☆ · PREP 25 MINS

Cantonese Lemon Chicken

Mirin has a much less, sharp flavour than wine vinegar, so I have used it in a few recipes in the book. It is well worth buying and will get used up in other recipes.

1½ mugs **basmati rice**

200g **mangetout**, each cut in half, lengthways

1 **egg**, beaten

3 **chicken breasts**, cut into bite-sized pieces

3 tablespoons **cornflour**

salt and **pepper**

3 teaspoons **5 spice powder**

2 tablespoons **sesame oil**

Sauce

juice of a **lemon**

1 tablespoon **sugar**

1 **GF chicken stock pot**

1 mug **water**

1 tablespoon **mirin**

1 tablespoon **cornflour**

1 Put the rice in 3 mugs of boiling water. Simmer for 12 minutes with a lid on the pan. Once cooked, remove from the heat and add the mangetout to the pan and leave, with the lid on, until needed.

2 Put the beaten egg in a bowl. Add the chicken.

3 Put the cornflour, salt and pepper and 5 spice on a large plate. Take the chicken out of the egg mixture and roll the pieces in the cornflour mix.

4 Heat the oil in a large frying pan and add the chicken pieces, separating them from each other. Fry for 4-5 minutes, turning frequently. Once the pieces are nicely browned, take out of the pan.

5 Mix the sauce ingredients together and add to the pan. Bring to the boil and then simmer for 1 minute, stirring all the time.

6 Serve the chicken on top of the rice and pour the sauce over.

Catalan Chicken with Creamy Polenta Mash

You may not have heard of Marsala wine, so you may be forgiven for thinking that this is one of those ingredients that you will buy and only use once. I have used it in quite a few recipes in this book. So, as it tastes delicious, I am sure it won't go to waste.

1 tablespoon **olive oil**

2 **onions**, sliced

3 **chicken breasts**, cut into bite-sized pieces

2 cloves **garlic**, finely chopped

1 tablespoon **GF flour**

3/4 mug/100g **raisins**

1 mug/300ml **Marsala wine**

1 mug/300ml **water**

1 tablespoon **GF liquid chicken stock**

3 tablespoons freshly chopped **parsley**

1/2 mug/50g **flaked almonds**

250g **cherry tomatoes**

Polenta

1 1/2 mugs/450ml **milk**

1 clove **garlic**, finely chopped

1/2 mug/100g **fine polenta**

1/2 mug/150ml **double cream**

1/2 mug/30g **grated Parmesan**

150g **mascarpone cheese**

1 Heat the oil in a large frying pan or wok. Add the onions and fry until they begin to soften.

2 Add the chicken breast and garlic and fry until the chicken is no longer pink on the outside.

3 Add the flour and mix together well. Add the raisins, Marsala, water and stockpot. Bring to the boil and simmer gently for 10 minutes.

4 Meanwhile, make the polenta. Put the milk, garlic, polenta and double cream in a medium saucepan, season and bring to the boil. Turn down the heat and cook for about 5 minutes, stirring frequently. The mixture will be very thick. Add the Parmesan and mascarpone and heat through. Set to one side until needed.

5 Add the parsley, almonds and tomatoes to the chicken and simmer for 1 minute.

6 Serve with the polenta.

Lightly Spiced Prawn & Lentil Salad with Warm Spiced Lentils

There are some unusual flavours here that make a delicious combination and an altogether healthy lunch. To deseed the cucumber, cut it in half lengthways and scoop out the seeds with a spoon, then slice.

2 tablespoons **pumpkin seeds**

1 teaspoon **fennel seeds**

2 tablespoons **olive oil**

1 ½ tablespoons freshly grated **ginger**

1 **onion**, chopped

1 clove **garlic**, finely chopped

400g tin **green lentils**

½ teaspoon **tumeric**

¼ teaspoon **ground cumin**

juice of a **lemon**

bag of **rocket leaves**

½ **cucumber**, deseeded and sliced

4 tablespoons **yoghurt**

handful of roughly chopped **fresh coriander**

500g **cooked prawns**

1 Toast the pumpkin and fennel seeds in a dry pan until they begin to pop. Take out of the pan and set to one side until needed.

2 Add the oil, ginger, onion, and garlic and fry for 2–3 minutes until the onion begins to soften.

3 Add the lentils, tumeric, cumin and lemon juice, simmer for 2 minutes and season.

4 Place the rocket leaves on the plates along with the cucumber and fresh coriander.

5 Sprinkle a tablespoon of yoghurt over the salad leaves. Layer over the warm lentils and the prawns. Sprinkle the toasted seeds on top and serve.

🌐 For a salad with a cheeky honey dressing, go to:
www.noshbooks.com/honey-dressing

Moroccan Minted Beef with Creamy Mash

We used to eat mince and mash when we were growing up, but it was nothing like this one. One thing that hasn't changed is that it is super cheap.

6 medium **potatoes**, peeled and cut into 2cm chunks

50g **butter**, measure using packet

2 tablespoons **single or double cream**

1 tablespoon **olive oil**

1 **onion**, sliced

2 cloves **garlic**, finely chopped

500g **minced beef**

2 teaspoons **cumin**

6 large **tomatoes**, chopped

1 tablespoon **tomato purée**

1 mug **water**

1 **GF beef stock cube**

2 tablespoons freshly chopped **mint**

2 tablespoons **toasted flaked almonds**

green beans

1 Put the potatoes in a pan of boiling water. Bring to the boil and then turn down to simmer for 10 minutes. Drain and return to the pan. Mash with the butter and the cream. Put the lid back on the pan and set to one side until needed.

2 Meanwhile, heat the oil in a large saucepan or wok. Add the onions and garlic and fry until the onion begins to soften. Add the beef and fry until no longer pink.

3 Add the cumin, tomatoes, tomato purée, water and stock cube. Bring to the boil and then turn down to simmer for 10 minutes.

4 Meanwhile, cook the green beans.

5 Add the mint and almonds. Mix together.

6 Serve with the creamy mash.

Leek & Ham Risotto

1 tablespoon **olive oil**

25g **butter**, measure using packet

1 small **red onion**, sliced

2 **leeks**, chopped

1 mug/175g **risotto rice**

2 mugs/600ml **water**

1 **GF chicken stock cube**

1 mug defrosted **frozen peas**

125g **cooked ham**, chopped

1/2 mug/25g **Parmesan**, grated

1 tablespoon roughly chopped **basil**

1 Heat the olive oil and butter in a wok or large frying pan. Add the onions and leeks and fry until they begin to soften.

2 Add the rice and fry for 1 minute to allow it to absorb the oils.

3 Add the water and the stock cube. Bring to the boil and then turn down to simmer, with a lid on the pan, for 10 minutes, or until the rice is tender. Add a little more water if necessary.

4 Season well and stir in the peas and the ham and gently heat for about 1 minute.

5 Stir in the Parmesan and allow to melt.

6 Season and sprinkle with the basil.

Curried Coconut Chicken

1 mug **rice**

4 **spring onions**, chopped

1 mug **frozen peas**, defrosted

1 tablespoon **oil**

1 **onion**, thinly sliced

1 **red pepper**, sliced

2 cloves **garlic**, finely chopped

2 tablespoons grated **fresh ginger**

3 **chicken breasts**, cut into bite-sized pieces

2 tablespoons **GF Korma curry paste**

2 tablespoons **GF soy sauce**

400ml **can coconut milk**

100g **mangetout**, cut into strips

handful of **coriander leaves**

1 Put the rice on to cook in 2 mugs of boiling water. Simmer for 12 minutes with the lid on the pan. Take off the heat then add the peas and spring onions, set aside with a lid on the pan.

2 Meanwhile, heat the oil in a wok and fry the onions, peppers, garlic and ginger. Fry until the onions begin to soften.

3 Add the chicken and fry until it is no longer pink on the outside.

4 Add the Korma paste, soy sauce and the coconut milk. Bring to the boil and then turn down to simmer for 3–4 minutes.

5 Add the mangetout and cook for a further minute.

6 Serve the coconut chicken with the rice and sprinkle the coriander leaves over the top.

Salmon Risotto with Crispy Parma Ham

25g **butter**, measure using packet

6 **spring onions**, chopped

3/4 mug **risotto rice**

1 1/2 mugs boiling **water**

1 dessertspoon **GF concentrated liquid veg stock** or 1/2 a **stock cube**

200g **sprouting broccoli**, thick stalks removed

3 **salmon fillets**

1 mug **frozen peas**, defrosted

70g **Parma ham**

1 Heat the butter in a frying pan, add the spring onions and fry for 30 seconds.

2 Add the rice and fry until it has absorbed the butter. Add the water and the stock. Bring to the boil and then turn down to simmer, with a lid over the pan, for 10 minutes. The rice should be almost soft by then.

3 Add the broccoli, cover the pan and leave for a further 5 minutes.

4 Cut the salmon into bite-sized chunks and add to the pan along with the peas. Put the lid on to cook for 3-4 minutes until the salmon is cooked. Season well.

5 Quickly fry the Parma ham in a separate frying pan. It will take not much more than a minute.

6 Serve the ham on top of the risotto.

Lemon & Dill Smoked Salmon Pasta

I love how the smoked salmon and dill give a fresh, but distinct, flavour to this dish. Combined with the lightness of the gluten-free pasta, it is a winner all round.

3 mugs **GF pasta**

150ml **crème fraîche**

juice of a **lemon**

2 x 200g **smoked salmon trimmings** or 2 x 125g packets of **smoked salmon**

1 tablespoon freshly chopped **dill**

6 **spring onions**, chopped

1 mug defrosted **frozen peas**.

1 Put the pasta in salted, boiling water, and simmer until tender. Drain, but reserve 1/2 mug of the cooking liquid. Return the pasta to the pan.

2 Add the rest of the ingredients, season and heat gently.

3 Add 1-2 tablespoons of the cooking liquid from the pasta, enough to make a loose sauce around the pasta. Serve immediately.

Spicy Sweet Potato & Chicken Curry

We have pictured it here with some poppadoms. Most poppadoms are gluten-free, but double check before you buy. They give a good, contrasting texture to the meal. You could even leave out the rice and just have poppadoms.

2 tablespoons **oil**

2 **sweet potatoes**, peeled and cut into 2cm pieces

2 tablespoons **GF rogan josh curry paste**

1/2 mug/120g **red lentils**

1 mug **water** + 1 **chicken stock cube**

400ml tin **coconut milk**

3 **chicken breasts**, cut into bite-sized pieces

200g bag **baby spinach leaves**

juice of a **lime**

1 **green chilli**, finely sliced

2 tablespoons freshly chopped **coriander**

1 1/2 mugs **basmati rice**

1 Heat the oil in a wok and add the sweet potatoes. Fry for 1 minute.

2 Add the curry paste and fry for 30 seconds.

3 Add the lentils, water, stock cube and the coconut milk. Simmer for 10 minutes or until the sweet potatoes are tender.

4 Add the chicken and simmer for 5-6 minutes. Check to make sure the chicken is cooked through.

5 Take off the heat and add the spinach, lime juice, chilli and coriander. Stir together and the spinach will wilt.

6 Serve with the rice.

Chicken with Plum Sauce & Flaked Almonds

A good alternative to takeaway and a guarantee of no additives. The mangetout add a good crunchy texture to the dish.

I searched and found that Kikkoman plum sauce is gluten-free.

1 ½ mugs **basmati rice**

2 tablespoons **sesame oil**

1 **red onion**, sliced

2 cloves **garlic**, chopped

1 small **leek**, sliced

3 **chicken breasts**, cut into bite-sized pieces

1/3 mug **water**

2 tablespoons **GF soy sauce**

4 tablespoons **GF hoisin sauce**

3 tablespoons **GF plum sauce**

100g **mangetout**, sliced lengthways

2 tablespoons **toasted flaked almonds**

1   Put the rice in 3 mugs of boiling water, bring to the boil and then turn down to simmer, with a lid on the pan, for 12 minutes. Leave in the pan and set to one side until needed.

2   Heat the oil in a wok. Add the onion, garlic and leeks and fry until the onion begins to soften.

3   Add the chicken and fry until it is no longer pink on the outside.

4   Add the water, soy sauce, hoisin sauce and plum sauce along with the mangetout. Bring to the boil and simmer for 1 minute.

5   Add the almonds and mix together.

6   Serve with the rice.

£ 1.80 /PERSON

SERVES 4

EASE ★★☆☆☆

PREP 15 MINS

Tarragon & Wholegrain Mustard Chicken

You may not have cooked with tarragon before, so this a great dish to try. This is a simple, everyday dish with plenty of flavour. You can take the mushroom rice idea and use with other dishes.

1 ½ mugs **basmati rice**

1 teaspoon **pilau rice seasoning**

1 tablespoon **olive oil**

3 **chicken breasts**, cut into bite-sized pieces

1 teaspoon **wholegrain mustard**

300ml **crème fraîche**

1 tablespoon freshly chopped **tarragon**

1 tablespoon **olive oil**

250g **chestnut mushrooms**, sliced

1   Put the rice in 3 mugs boiling water, add the pilau rice seasoning and bring to the boil. Turn down to simmer for 12 minutes with a lid on the pan. Set to one side until needed.

2   Heat 1 tablespoon of oil in a frying pan and fry the chicken pieces until they begin to brown. Add the mustard and cook for 30 seconds. Add the crème fraîche and the chopped tarragon and allow to simmer for 1 minute. Season well.

3   Heat the other tablespoon of oil in another frying pan and fry the mushrooms until they begin to brown. Season well. Add the rice to the pan and stir well, allowing it to fry for 1 minute.

🌐 See another pan-fried chicken recipe online:
www.noshbooks.com/spiced-chicken

Cider & Cranberry Bangers with Mash

Gluten-free sausages are now available at most supermarkets. The good thing is that they don't get packed out with loads of breadcrumbs and are therefore full of flavour.

5-6 **potatoes**, unpeeled and cut into 2cm cubes

25g **butter**, measure using packet

1 tablespoon **olive oil**

8 **GF sausages**

1 **onion**, sliced

1 tablespoon **GF flour**

440ml can **cider**

1 teaspoon **light brown sugar**

100g **cranberries**

green beans

1 Put the potatoes into boiling salted water. Bring to the boil and then simmer for 10 minutes. Drain and return to the pan, add the butter and crush. Set to one side, with a lid on the pan, until needed.

2 Meanwhile, heat the oil in a large frying pan and fry the sausages on a medium heat. When the sausages are almost cooked, add the onions and fry until browned.

3 Put the beans in a pan of boiling salted water and then simmer for 5 minutes. Once they are cooked, drain and return to the pan.

4 Once the sausages are cooked, remove them from the pan. Add the flour to the pan and mix well. Add the cider, sugar and the cranberries. Bring to the boil, stirring frequently; the sauce should thicken. Return the sausages and onions to the pan and heat through for 1 minute.

5 Serve with the mash and beans.

Mango Chicken Quinoa Salad

Sweet, sticky, caramelised strips of chicken. What more can you say?

1 mug **quinoa**

Marinade
2 tablespoons **mango chutney**
juice of a **lime**
1 tablespoon **GF Korma curry paste**
salt and **pepper**

3 **chicken breasts**, cut into strips
1 tablespoon **olive oil**

Salad
1/2 **cucumber**, diced
1 bunch **spring onions**, chopped
10 **ready-to-eat dried apricots**, chopped
2 tablespoons freshly chopped **mint**
125g **cherry tomatoes**, halved

1. Put the quinoa in half a pan of boiling water and simmer for 15 minutes.

2. Mix the marinade ingredients together and add the chicken. Leave for 5 minutes. Heat 1 tablespoon oil in a large frying pan and add the chicken. Fry on a medium heat for 5–6 minutes, being careful not to burn the marinade. Add the rest of the marinade and allow to bubble for 1 minute. If the sauce goes too thick, add 2 tablespoons water.

3. Mix the salad ingredients together and share amongst the plates. Serve the chicken on top and pour over a little of the sauce.

TESTER #4

Christine

I have been gluten-free for 16 years and I miss granary bread!

I tried the 'Mango Chicken Quinoa Salad', delicious, served to friends and family of all ages, a good balance of flavours, and consistently appreciated: everyone cleared their plates. I was intimidated by quinoa and, thanks to this book, have finally worked out how to use it!

Cheat's Egg Fried Rice with Chicken & Prawns

Don't think of takeaway egg fried rice; this is nothing like it. Truly a dish in its own right.

1 mug **basmati rice**

2 tablespoons **toasted sesame oil**

3 **large eggs**, beaten

6 **spring onions**, sliced

2 **chicken breasts**, cut into thin slices

250g **cooked prawns**

2 **pak choi**, thinly sliced

4 tablespoons **GF oyster sauce**

1 Put the rice on to cook in 2 mugs boiling water. Bring to the boil and then turn down to simmer, with a lid on the pan, for 12 minutes. Take off the heat and set to one side until needed.

2 Heat 1 tablespoon of the oil in a wok. Add the egg and swish around so that it makes a thin omelette, Once set, tip out of the wok onto a plate until it has cooled, then roll up and cut into slices.

3 Meanwhile, heat the other tablespoon of oil in the wok and add the onions and chicken. Fry until the chicken is no longer pink.

4 Add the prawns and pak choi and fry for 2 minutes.

5 Add the oyster sauce and the cooked rice and heat everything through. Should take about a minute. Season and serve.

Coconut Cod on a Pea & Broccoli Mash

It may seem a bit strange to put coconut with fish, but this one really works. The coconut gives a lovely, crunchy coating as well.

Mash

4 medium **potatoes**, peeled and cut into 2cm chunks

1 small head **broccoli**, stalk chopped and head cut into florets

2 mugs defrosted **frozen peas**

25g **butter**, measure using packet

4 **cod fillets**

1 beaten **egg**

4 tablespoons **desiccated coconut**

olive oil to fry

Sauce

juice of a **lemon**

4 tablespoons **light brown sugar**

2 tablespoons **water**

1 Put the potatoes and broccoli stalks into a pan of salted boiling water, bring to the boil, then turn down to simmer for 5 minutes. Add the broccoli florets and the peas and simmer for a further 5 minutes. Drain and mash roughly with the butter.

2 Season the beaten eggs, dip in the cod fillets and then dip them into the coconut. Heat the oil in a frying pan and cook the cod on a medium heat until the fish is browned on the outside and cooked through. Should take about 5 minutes, depending on the thickness of the fish.

3 Remove the fish from the pan, add the sauce ingredients and season. Allow to simmer for 2 minutes. The sauce should thicken slightly.

4 Serve with the fish and the mash.

These recipes are all quick to prepare, but just need a bit of time in the oven to cook. Sit down and have a cuppa while you wait for your dinner to develop.

Gavin

I'm a rugby player and personal trainer (GWD Performance) and I'm currently studying a sports and exercise science degree. I first started to cut down on gluten about 3-4 years ago as I started to learn more about nutrition, and the effects gluten can have on the body. Cutting out bread was the hardest and I admit I do have it every now and then, but when I do have anything with gluten in it now my stomach plays havoc, as it is now used to not having it that much. I'm not gluten intolerant so to speak, but everyone is to a certain extent.

I think this is a great cookbook as it shows you that healthy food can also be tasty, contrary to a lot of peoples beliefs. I will definitely be recommending this book to my clients as it is all about eating real, unprocessed food, which is what I try to hammer home to my clients all the time.

Puy Lentils & Roast Vegetables with Lemon Chicken

Puy lentils are grown in the region of La Puy. The rich volcanic soil gives the lentils an earthy flavour. They are also a great source of protein.

Roasted veg

2 **sweet potatoes**, diced

3 **white potatoes**, diced

2 **courgettes**, diced

2 tablespoons **olive oil**

2 tablespoons **olive oil**

2 **onions**, sliced

2 cloves **garlic**, finely chopped

3 **chicken breasts**, cut into bite-sized pieces

2 tablespoons **GF flour**

2 teaspoons **paprika**

1 teaspoon **turmeric**

1 teaspoon **cumin seeds**

1/2 **lemon** cut into thin rounds

2 mugs **water**

1 **GF chicken stock cube**

400g tin **puy lentils**, rinsed and drained

2 tablespoons freshly chopped **coriander**

1 Preheat the oven to 200°C fan oven/220°C/ gas 7. Chop the veg into 2cm chunks. Place on a roasting tray, sprinkle with olive oil and season. Place in the oven for 35 minutes.

2 Heat the oil in a large frying pan or wok. Add the onions and garlic and fry until the onions begin to soften. Add the chicken and fry until no longer pink.

3 Add the flour and the spices, mix well and fry for 30 seconds. Add the lemon, water and the stock cube, season well and bring to the boil. Turn down to simmer for 10 minutes.

4 Add the lentils and the coriander and serve with the roast veg.

Try our 'Spiced Chicken with Puy Lentils' recipe: www.noshbooks.com/puy

£2.00 /PERSON

SERVES 4

EASE ★★★☆☆

PREP 20 MINS

COOK 15 MINS

OK TO FREEZE

Tortilla Layered Beef & Bean Pie

I suppose you could say this is a Mexican twist on the more traditional lasagna, but it is much simpler and quicker to make.

1 tablespoon **olive oil**

1 **onion**, chopped

500g **minced beef**

1 **clove garlic**, chopped

6 large **tomatoes**, chopped

1 **fat red chilli**, chopped

420g **tin cannellini beans**, rinsed and drained

1 tablespoon **tomato purée**

1 **GF beef stock cube** in ¼ mug **hot water**

1 tablespoon freshly chopped **basil**

6 **GF tortillas**

1½ mugs grated **cheese**

300ml tub **soured cream** to serve

salad leaves

1 Preheat the oven to 200°C fan oven/220°C/gas 7. Grease a large casserole dish or roasting tray.

2 Heat the oil in a large saucepan or wok. Fry the onion until it begins to soften. Add the mince and cook until no longer pink.

3 Add the garlic, tomatoes, chilli, beans, tomato purée and stock cube and water. Season well and bring to the boil. Simmer for 10 minutes. Add the basil.

4 Lay a tortilla on the roasting tray, put ⅕ of the mince mixture on top and then sprinkle some of the cheese on the top. Lay the next tortilla and repeat. Sprinkle the last of cheese on the top. Add a few dollops of soured cream and sprinkle over some paprika.

5 Put in the oven for 15 minutes or until the cheese melts and browns a little.

6 Cut into slices and serve with the soured cream and salad leaves.

Polenta & Parmesan Coated Chicken Nuggets

These chicken nuggets beat any gluten laden, ready-made ones that you can buy. The Parmesan gives them a crunchy, tasty outside, whilst the chicken in the centre is still nice and tender.

5 medium **potatoes**, unpeeled and cut into 2cm chunks

2 tablespoons **olive oil**

1/2 mug **fine polenta**

1/2 mug finely grated **Parmesan**

3 **chicken breasts**

1 **egg**, beaten

Sauce

3 tablespoons **mayo**

10 **green olives**, chopped

juice of 1/2 **lemon**

salt and **pepper**

1 Preheat the oven, 180°C fan oven/200°C/gas 6.

2 Put the potatoes on a large baking tray. Sprinkle over the oil and season well. Distribute everything well with your hands and spread out the potatoes. Place in the oven for 30 minutes, or until nicely browned.

3 Put the polenta and Parmesan on a large plate and season. Cut the chicken into nugget-sized pieces. Put the beaten egg into a bowl. Dip the chicken pieces first in the egg and then into the polenta mix. Place on a greased baking tray and bake in the oven for 20 minutes.

4 Mix the sauce ingredients together.

5 Serve with the mini roasts and the sauce.

£1.21 /PERSON · SERVES 4 · EASE ★★☆☆☆ · PREP 30 MINS · COOK 3 MINS · V

Tortilla Topped Veggie Bake

1 **sweet potato**, peeled and cut into 2cm chunks

1 small head of **broccoli**, broken into florets

1 tablespoon **olive oil**

1 **onion**, sliced

1 **red pepper**, chopped

5 **mushrooms**, sliced

1 **courgette**, cut into chunks

1 tablespoon **GF soy sauce**

Sauce

25g **butter**, measure using the packet

2 tablespoons **GF flour**

1 1/2 mugs **milk**

1 mug grated **cheese**

salt and **pepper**

100g packet **GF corn tortillas**

1 mug grated **Cheddar cheese**

1 Preheat the grill.

2 Put the sweet potato into a pan of boiling water, bring to the boil and simmer for 5 minutes. Add the broccoli and simmer for a further 5 minutes. Drain and return to the pan. Set to one side until needed.

3 Heat the oil in a wok and fry the onions and peppers until the onion begins to soften. Add the mushrooms and courgettes until they begin to brown. Add the soy, sweet potatoes and broccoli. Mix together and pour into a large casserole dish.

4 Melt the butter in a saucepan and add the flour. Cook for 30 seconds. Add the milk and cheese and bring to the boil, stirring frequently, until the sauce thickens. Season and pour over the veggies.

5 Put the tortilla chips on top and sprinkle the cheese over. Place under the grill for 2–3 minutes or until the cheese melts and the chips begin to brown.

Olla Podrida with Polenta Chips

In this recipe we are using a ready-made polenta. If you want, you can make your own, see page 144. It stores really well in the freezer. An Olla Podrida is traditionally a Spanish stew with beans and sausages. You can add a little spice if you want to mix it up a little. Try a teaspoon of paprika or a chopped chilli.

Polenta chips

3 tablespoons **olive oil**

2 x 500g packet of **ready-made polenta**

1 mug grated **Parmesan**

6 **GF sausages**

1 tablespoon **olive oil**

1 **onion**, sliced

1 **red pepper**, cut into small chunks

2 cloves **garlic**, chopped finely

1 sprig **rosemary**, leaves stripped off and chopped

400g can **adzuki beans**, rinsed and drained

400g can **butter beans**, rinsed and drained

250g **cherry tomatoes**

1 mug/300ml **water**

1 **GF beef stock cube**

2 tablespoons **tomato purée**

1 Preheat the oven to 200°C fan oven/220°C/ gas 7. Put the oil on a large roasting tray. Cut the polenta into chunky chips, put on the roasting tray and roll in the oil. Season and then sprinkle over the Parmesan. Place in the oven for 35 minutes, or until the chips are lightly browned.

2 Meanwhile, slit the sausage skins lengthways with a sharp knife and take off the skins. Pinch each sausage into 4 pieces; no need to roll into balls. Heat the oil in a wok and fry until the sausages become browned on all sides. Remove from the wok and set to one side.

3 Add the onions, peppers, garlic and rosemary and fry until the onions begin to soften.

4 Add the rest of the ingredients and return the sausages to the wok. Simmer for 15 minutes.

5 Serve with the polenta chips.

£ 2.37 /PERSON   SERVES 4   EASE ★★☆☆☆   PREP 25 MINS   COOK 5 MINS

Leek & Ham Parmesan Pasta Bake

Here, the creamy pesto sauce and the crunchy breadcrumb topping make a fantastic combination of tastes and textures.

3 mugs **GF pasta**

Sauce

25g **butter**, measure using packet

1 teaspoon **GF flour**

1 mug/300ml **milk**

185g **GF pesto**

50g **butter**, measure using the packet

2 **leeks**, chopped

240g **sliced ham**, chopped roughly

1/2 mug grated **Parmesan**

1 slice **GF bread**, made into breadcrumbs

1 Cook the pasta, drain and return to the pan.

2 Heat the 25g butter in a saucepan, add the flour and cook until the mixture begins to bubble slightly. Add the milk and bring to the boil, stirring all the time. Add the pesto and set to one side.

3 Heat the 50g butter in a wok or large saucepan, add the leeks and fry until they begin to brown.

4 Preheat the grill.

5 Add the ham, sauce, leeks and pasta to the large pan and mix together. Season well.

6 Pour out into a large casserole dish. Spread the breadcrumbs over the top and sprinkle over the Parmesan. Place under the grill for about 5 minutes, or until the top browns slightly.

Cottage Pie
with a Rustic Leek & Potato Top

This is probably the fastest cottage pie I have ever made. Here, there is no need to peel the potatoes, always a plus for me, and you still end up with a crispy top.

1 tablespoon **olive oil**

1 **onion**, chopped

2 cloves **garlic**, chopped

500g **minced beef**

2 tablespoons **GF plain flour**

1 sprig **rosemary**

1 1/2 mugs **water**

1 **GF beef stock cube**

5 **medium potatoes**, cut into 2cm chunks

25g **butter**, measure using packet

2 **leeks**, chopped

1   Preheat the oven to 200°C fan oven/220°C/gas 7.

2   Heat the oil in a large frying pan or wok. Add the onion and garlic and fry until it begins to soften. Add the mince and fry until it is no longer pink.

3   Add the flour and mix well. Add the rosemary, water and the stock cube. Mix together and bring to the boil, stirring frequently. Season well and turn down to simmer for 10 minutes.

4   Put the potatoes on to simmer for 10 minutes. Drain and return to the pan.

5   Put the butter in a frying pan and fry the leeks until they begin to brown. Add to the drained potatoes and mix.

6   Pour the meat into a casserole dish and arrange the leek and potato mix over the top. Bake in the oven for 15 minutes. The top should be lightly browned.

Pork Enchiladas with Apple Salsa

A simple dish for friends around. The old combo of pork and apple works every time. Again, be careful that the corn tortillas are actually gluten-free (see page 8).

1 tablespoon **olive oil**

500g **pork mince**

1 **fat red chilli**, deseeded and chopped

3 teaspoons **coriander**

3 teaspoons **cumin**

1 teaspoon **GF plain flour**

1/2 mug/150ml **water**

Salsa

4 **spring onions**

250g **cherry tomatoes**, chopped

1 **apple**, cored and chopped

1 tablespoon **olive oil**

juice of a **lime**

8 **GF corn tortillas**

Topping

300ml **soured cream**

1/2 mug grated **cheese**

1/2 teaspoons **paprika**

1 Preheat the oven to 180°C fan oven/200°C/gas 6. Grease a medium-sized casserole dish.

2 Heat the oil in a frying pan. Add the mince and fry until it is no longer pink. Add the chilli, spices and flour. Mix well. Add the water and simmer for 1 minute.

3 Mix the salsa ingredients together.

4 Divide the meat between the tortillas, add the salsa and roll them up. Place together in the casserole dish.

5 Pour over the soured cream. Sprinkle the cheese and the paprika over the top.

6 Place in the oven for 15-20 minutes. The cheese should be melted and lightly browned.

Minted Lamb Pie

When making the pastry, if you don't have a processor, rub the butter into the flour with your fingertips until it resembles breadcrumbs. Gluten-free pastry is very delicate. I find the best way to handle it is to roll it out on some floured cling film, use this to flip it over the rolling pin and then on to the top of the pie.

1 tablespoon **olive oil**

1 **onion**, sliced

4 medium **carrots**, diced

500g **minced lamb**

2 tablespoons **GF plain flour**

2 mugs **water**

GF lamb stock cube

2 tablespoons freshly chopped **mint**

Shortcrust Pastry

2 mugs/360g **GF plain flour**

1 teaspoon **xanthan gum**

1/2 teaspoon **salt**

175g **butter**, measure using packet

1 egg + 1/3 mug **cold water**

6 medium **potatoes**

green veg

1　Preheat the oven 180°C fan oven/200°C/gas 6.

2　Heat the oil in a frying pan or large saucepan. Add the onion and carrots and fry until the onion begins to soften.

3　Add the mince and fry until no longer pink. Add the flour and mix well. Add the water and stock, season and bring to the boil. Simmer for 10 minutes.

4　Meanwhile, put the flour, xanthan gum, salt and butter in a processor. Whizz until the mixture resembles breadcrumbs. Add the egg and water and pulse the processor until a soft dough is formed. Turn out onto a floured surface and roll out until it is just under 1cm thick.

5　Add the mint to the meat and pour into a casserole dish. Wet the top edges of the dish with water. Carefully lift the pastry onto the rolling pin and then spread over the meat. Trim the edges and crimp them. Brush the top with beaten egg. Make a hole in the centre to let the steam out.

6　Place in the oven for 35-40 minutes. Serve with mash and green veg.

Tuna Arrabbiata

Arrabbiata is a spicy Italian pasta sauce made from tomatoes, garlic and red chillies. Arrabbiata means 'angry' in Italian, so, presumably, we have an angry sauce here! Not too hot though.

3 mugs **GF pasta**

1 tablespoon **olive oil**

1 **red** and 1 **yellow pepper**, chopped

2 cloves **garlic**, chopped finely

1 **fat red chilli**, chopped finely

8 large **tomatoes**, chopped

20 **black or green olives**

2 x 185g tins **tuna**

1/2 mug grated **Parmesan**

1 Put the pasta on to cook.

2 Meanwhile, heat the oil in a large frying pan or hob to oven casserole. Fry the peppers until they begin to brown.

3 Preheat the grill.

4 Add the garlic and chillies and cook for 30 seconds. Add the tomatoes and olives and cook for 2 minutes. Season with salt and pepper.

5 Drain the pasta and stir into the pan along with the flaked tuna. Gently mix together. Sprinkle the Parmesan over the top and place under the grill for about 5 minutes, until the cheese bubbles and begins to brown.

Beef Cobbler

This is a good one-pot dish to make if you have a hob to oven casserole dish.

2 tablespoons **olive oil**

1 **onion**, sliced

3 medium **carrots**, sliced

500g **minced beef**

2 tablespoons **GF flour**

6 **tomatoes**, roughly chopped

2 mugs **water**

1 **GF beef stock cube**

Cobblers

1 mug/125g **fine cornmeal**

2/3 mug/100g **GF self-raising flour**

1 teaspoon **GF baking powder**

1 teaspoon **xanthan gum**

2 tablespoons freshly chopped **herbs** (**basil** and **parsley**)

100g **butter**, measure using packet

1 **egg** + 1/4 mug **water**

1 **egg**, beaten

green veg to serve

1   Preheat the oven 180°C fan oven/200°C/gas 6.

2   Heat the oil in a hob to oven casserole. Add the onions and carrots and fry until the onion begins to soften.

3   Add the beef and fry until no longer pink. Add the flour and mix well.

4   Add the tomatoes, water and stock cube and season. Bring to the boil and then simmer for 10 minutes.

5   Meanwhile, make the cobbler. Put the cornmeal, flour, baking powder, xanthan gum, herbs, butter and seasoning in a food processor. Whizz for 2 minutes and you should have something resembling breadcrumbs. Add the egg and water and pulse a few times until it forms a dough. Take out of the processor and form into 8 balls. Squash each one down a little and place them on top of the beef. Brush each one with beaten egg.

6   Place in the oven for 25 minutes. Serve with some green veg.

£ 1.72 /PERSON SERVES 4-5 EASE ★★★★☆ PREP 25 MINS COOK 50 MINS OK TO FREEZE

Crunchy Topped Lasagna

1 tablespoon **olive oil**

1 **onion**, chopped

1 **carrot**, chopped

2 **celery sticks**

2 **cloves garlic**, finely chopped

500g **beef mince**

100g **pancetta lardons**

1 sprig **rosemary**

2 **bay leaves**

1 tablespoon **maple syrup**

1 mug **water**

1 **GF beef stock cube**

2 tablespoons **tomato purée**

6 large **tomatoes**, chopped

10-12 **GF lasagna** sheets

2 slices **GF bread**, made into breadcrumbs

1/2 mug grated **Parmesan**

White sauce

2 mugs **milk**

2 tablespoons **cornflour**

1/2 mug grated **Cheddar cheese**

50g **butter**, measure using packet

1 Heat the oil in a large frying pan or wok. Add the onion, carrot, celery and garlic and fry for 3 minutes.

2 Add the beef and pancetta and fry until the mince is no longer pink.

3 Add the rosemary, bay leaves, maple syrup, water, stock cube, tomato purée and tomatoes. Bring to the boil, season with salt and pepper and then turn down to simmer for 15 minutes. Remove the bay leaves and rosemary.

4 Make the white sauce by mixing the milk and cornflour together, add the cheese and butter and season. Heat in a small saucepan and gently bring to the boil. The sauce should thicken. Set to one side until needed.

5 Preheat the oven to 180°C/200°C/gas 7.

6 Grease a large casserole dish and layer in this order, meat sauce, lasagna sheets, white sauce, lasagna sheets and repeat. You should have enough mixture for 2 layers of each, with a layer of meat sauce on the top.

7 Mix the breadcrumbs and Parmesan together and sprinkle over the top.

8 Place in the oven for 35 minutes. Turn the oven down to 160°C fan oven/180°C/gas 5 and cook for a further 15 minutes. The top should be browned and crunchy and the pasta tender.

Pan Fried Polenta Wedges
with Chorizo & Red Pepper Sauce

Ready-made polenta is available at Tesco, but not always in other supermarkets. Making it yourself it really easy and not too time consuming and it also freezes quite well.

Polenta

1 mug of **fine polenta**

4 mugs **boiling water**

3 **GF veg stock pots**

3/4 mug grated **Parmesan cheese**

1 tablespoon **olive oil** to fry

(you can use 500g packet of ready-made polenta if you like)

1 tablespoon **olive oil**

1 **onion**, sliced

1 **red pepper**, chopped

200g **chorizo**, sliced

2 cloves **garlic**, chopped

4 **tomatoes**, roughly chopped

2 tablespoons freshly chopped **basil**

1 Put the boiling water and stock pots in a medium saucepan. Add the polenta and stir well. Simmer for 10 minutes, stirring frequently. The polenta will be quite thick.

2 Season and add the cheese, stirring until it melts. Pour into a greased 20 x 30cm tray and leave to cool. Store in the fridge until needed.

3 Cut the polenta into wedges. Heat the oil in a large frying pan and fry the polenta on each side until it is nicely browned; takes about 3-4 minutes each side.

4 Heat the other tablespoon of oil in another frying pan or wok, add the onions and peppers and fry until they begin to brown. Add the chorizo and fry until they begin to brown.

5 Add the garlic and tomatoes and season well. Cook for 2-3 minutes and then add the basil.

£ 1.81 /PERSON · SERVES 4 · EASE ★★★☆☆ · PREP 25 MINS · COOK 50 MINS

Chicken Provencal with Boulangerie Potatoes

5 medium **potatoes**, cut into ½ cm slices

2 tablespoons **olive oil**

½ mug **water**

Sauce

juice of a **lemon**

2 tablespoons **olive oil**

2 tablespoons **GF soy sauce**

1 tablespoon **GF Worcestershire sauce**

1 tablespoon **honey**

1 tablespoon **tomato purée**

1 tablespoon **wholegrain mustard**

6 **tomatoes**, roughly chopped

1 tablespoon **olive oil**

8 rashers **bacon**

3 **chicken breasts**

25 **black olives**, roughly chopped

2 tablespoons freshly chopped **parsley**

2 tablespoons **crème fraîche**

1 Preheat the oven to 200°C fan oven/220°C/gas 7.

2 Put the sliced potatoes, oil and water in a large roasting tin. Arrange so they are flat and season well. Place in the oven for 45 minutes.

3 Meanwhile, put the sauce ingredients in a food processor and blitz till quite smooth. Season and set to one side until needed.

4 Heat the oil in a large frying pan and fry the bacon until crisp. Take out of the pan and drain on some kitchen paper. Cut into bite-sized pieces.

5 Cut the chicken into large pieces. Add to the frying pan and fry on each side for 2 minutes. Add the sauce and bacon to the pan, bring to the boil and simmer for 5 minutes with a lid on the pan. Stir in the olives, parsley and crème fraîche.

6 The potatoes should be nicely browned. Serve with the chicken.

SERVES 4

EASE ★★☆☆☆

PREP 20 MINS

COOK 5 MINS

Rich & Creamy Salmon Pie

Delightful fish pie with a smooth and creamy cheese sauce. Only takes 25 minutes in total. So this is super quick, considering it's a pie!

5 **large potatoes**, peeled and cut into 2cm chunks

50g **butter**, measure using packet

Cheese sauce

2 mugs grated **Cheddar cheese**

3 tablespoons **GF flour**

2 mugs **milk**

3 **salmon fillets** approx 400g, cut into bite-sized pieces

1 mug **frozen peas**, defrosted

1 bunch **spring onions**, chopped

1 tablespoon freshly chopped **basil**

1 tablespoon freshly chopped **parsley**

1 Boil the potatoes for about 10 minutes. Drain and mash with the butter.

2 Meanwhile, put the cheese and flour in a large saucepan and mix together. Add the milk and season well. Bring to the boil, stirring frequently. You should have a thickened sauce.

3 Add the fish, peas, spring onions and herbs and heat through until the fish is cooked. Should take 2-3 minutes.

4 Preheat the grill.

5 Pour the fish mixture in the bottom of an ovenproof casserole and spread the mash over the top. Place under the grill for 5 minutes or so until the top is nicely browned.

138 pop it in the oven

Spinach & Prawn Gruyère Gratin

The Gruyère cheese brings a sweetness to this dish, so it is really not worth substituting Cheddar in its place.

2 mugs **GF pasta**

Sauce
100g grated **Gruyère cheese**
1 tablespoon **GF flour**
1 mug/300ml **single cream**
1 mug **milk**

400g **cooked prawns**
200g chopped **fresh spinach**
100g grated **Gruyère cheese**

1 Preheat the grill.

2 Put the pasta on to cook. Drain and return to the pan.

3 Meanwhile, put 100g of the cheese and the flour in a large saucepan and mix together. Add the cream and milk and season well. Gently bring to the boil, stirring frequently; the sauce should thicken.

4 Add the prawns and spinach and cook through; should take 2 minutes or so. Mix in the drained pasta.

5 Tip into an ovenproof casserole dish and sprinkle the rest of the cheese over the top. Place under the grill until the cheese bubbles and browns slightly. Should take about 5 minutes.

Just a few ideas, some quick and easy and some that may take a little more time. Hope these ideas help you, especially if you have bought this book to cook for your gluten-free friends.

TESTER #6

Sarah

I'm a full time Mum, married to Andrew and we have 3 boys, Joe (13), Freddie (9) and Billy (4). I am also studying for a degree in Childhood and Youth Studies.

Since going GF 2 years ago, my IBS symptoms settled down almost immediately, certainly after 2 weeks of being gluten-free, and I haven't looked back.

When I tried the 'Minted Lamb Pie' - I am so pleased to say that from this recipe I was actually able to make a decent shortcrust pastry. I have tried before, but it was far too crumbly. This pastry held up well and I couldn't get enough of it.

'Polenta and Parmesan Coated Chicken Nuggets' - I made these for the children and one of their friends who'd come over for tea. They went down a storm and my son, who claims to hate polenta, was shocked when I told him what he'd been eating.

Good Ol' Posh Steak Dinner with Parmesan Polenta Chips

Polenta Chips

1 mug **fine polenta**

4 mugs **boiling water**

3 **GF veg stock pots**

3/4 mug grated **Parmesan**

olive oil to roast

Caramelised onion and red pepper sauce

1 tablespoon **olive oil**

25g **butter**, measure using packet

1 **red onion**, sliced

1 **red pepper**, sliced

1 **garlic clove**, chopped finely

1 tablespoon **GF flour**

1 teaspoon **paprika**

1/2 **GF beef stock cube**

1 mug **water**

150g **cherry tomatoes**

purple sprouting broccoli

2 **rump steaks**

1 teaspoon **paprika**

1 teaspoon **dried thyme**

olive oil to fry

1 To make the polenta, add the polenta to the boiling water and stir well. Add the veg stock pots and season. Bring to the boil and then simmer for 10 minutes, stirring all the time. The polenta will be quite thick. Add the Parmesan and stir until it melts. Pour into a greased 20 x 30cm traybake tin and leave to set. It takes about 1 1/2 hours. Cut into large chip shapes. Place on a roasting tray with about 2 tablespoons of olive oil. Roll the chips in the oil to cover all sides. Place in a preheated oven (200°C fan oven/220°C/gas 7) for 40-45 minutes. The chips should be nicely browned.

2 To make the sauce, heat the oil and butter in a frying pan, add the onions and pepper and fry on a medium heat until everything begins to brown. Turn down the heat and cook until everything is really browned and caramelised. Add the garlic and fry for 1 minute. Add the flour and the paprika and cook for 30 seconds. Add the stock and water and bring to the boil. Add the tomatoes and cook for 1 minute. Season well.

3 Put the broccoli on to cook, simmering for 4-5 minutes.

4 On a plate, mix the paprika, thyme, salt and pepper. Rub into the steak. Heat the oil in a frying pan on quite a high heat. Cook the steaks for 2 minutes each side and you will have rare steaks, 2 minutes each side again on a medium heat and you will have medium rare. Serve everything together and enjoy.

Marsala & Paprika Chicken

I have consistently used Marsala in this book. This means you are not having to buy lots of different wines and spirits. One bottle will last for ages and not 'go off'. I find it a lovely, rich wine to cook with.

Rice

1 1/2 mugs **basmati rice**

3 **chicken breasts**

2 teaspoons **paprika**

salt and **pepper**

1 tablespoon **olive oil**

2 tablespoons **olive oil**

250g pack **chestnut mushrooms**, sliced

bunch **spring onions**, chopped

1 tablespoon freshly chopped **basil**

1 tablespoon freshly chopped **parsley**

Sauce

300ml **Marsala wine**

1/2 mug/150ml **double cream**

1   Put the rice in a pan with 3 mugs boiling water. Bring to the boil and then turn down to simmer for 12 minutes. Once cooked, set to one side until needed.

2   Meanwhile, put the chicken breasts in a sandwich bag or some cling film and give it a bit of a bash with a rolling pin to flatten it out. Put the paprika and salt and pepper on a large plate and then press the chicken breast into it. Heat 1 tablespoon of oil in a frying pan and fry the chicken for 3 minutes each side on a medium heat. Remove from the pan and leave to rest. Cut into strips.

3   Meanwhile, in a wok, heat the 2 tablespoons of oil. Add the mushrooms and spring onions and fry until the mushrooms begin to brown. Season well and then add to the cooked rice along with the herbs and mix.

4   Add the Marsala to the chicken pan and allow to boil gently for 2 minutes, or until it is reduced by half. Add the cream and heat through gently.

Salmon with Pak Choi Rice & Lemon Ginger Sauce

Sumptuous, just-cooked salmon steak, with a fresh lemon and ginger sauce. Brilliant for friends around.

1 mug **rice**

3 **pak choi**, thinly sliced

Sauce

25g **butter**, measure using packet

6 **spring onions**, chopped

1 tablespoon finely chopped **ginger**

2 tablespoons freshly chopped **parsley**

1 tablespoon **runny honey**

1 teaspoon **cornflour** mixed into 1/2 mug **water**

juice of a **lemon**

1 tablespoon **toasted sesame oil**

4 **salmon fillets**

1 Put the rice on to cook in 2 mugs of boiling water. When cooked, take off the heat and add the pack choi to the pan, replace the lid and leave for 2 minutes. The pak choi will cook in the steam from the rice. Mix together.

2 Meanwhile, heat the butter in a small saucepan, add the onions and ginger and fry for 1 minute. Add the rest of the sauce ingredients and bring to the boil, the sauce should thicken. Season.

3 Heat the sesame oil in a medium frying pan, add the salmon steaks, season well and fry on each side for 2–3 minutes. They should be crispy on the outside and just cooked in the centre.

4 Serve with the rice and the sauce.

🌐 Here is another idea for using salmon:
www.noshbooks.com/posh-salmon

Chicken Milanese with Avocado Salad & Pan Roast Potatoes

Great meal to make when you have friends around. Get all the ingredients prepared before they come, so you won't be running around in the kitchen when you want to be chatting. You can roast the potatoes in the oven, takes about 30 minutes at 180ºC fan oven/200ºC/gas 6. Makes one less thing to do when folks arrive.

1 tablespoon **olive oil**

5 medium **potatoes**, cut into small cubes

2 **Cos lettuce**, sliced

2 **avocados** , peeled and chopped into 1cm cubes

4 **tomatoes**, chopped

bunch **spring onions**, chopped

Dressing

2 tablespoons **olive oil**

2 tablespoons **honey**

juice of a **lemon**

salt and **pepper**

4 medium **chicken breasts**

1 **egg**, beaten

3 slices **GF bread**, made into breadcrumbs

1 tablespoon **olive oil**

1 Heat the oil in a frying pan. Add the potatoes and fry on a medium heat, with a lid on the pan, for about 15 minutes. Turn the potatoes frequently during that time to ensure that they brown evenly.

2 Meanwhile, prepare the salad and the dressing. Don't mix together until just before serving.

3 Put the chicken breasts between a couple of pieces of cling film, give them a good bash with a rolling pin to flatten them and season with salt and pepper. Put the beaten egg in a bowl and dip the chicken breast in it. Put the breadcrumbs on a plate and press the chicken pieces into them.

4 Heat the oil in a frying pan and fry the chicken for 4 minutes each side on a medium heat. Take care not to burn the breadcrumbs.

5 Serve the chicken with the potatoes and salad.

£3.08 /PERSON · SERVES 6 · EASE ★★★★★ · PREP 25 MINS · COOK 40 MINS · OK TO FREEZE

Salmon en Croûte
with a Dijon Crème Fraîche

Gluten-free pastry, along with bread, is one of the more difficult things to make with non-wheat flour, as it is very 'short'. I have suggested using cling film to help in moving it around and have found it works well.

2 mugs/360g **GF self-raising flour**

1 teaspoon **xanthan gum**

175g **butter**, measure using packet

1 **egg** + 1/3 mug **water**

1 large **salmon fillet**, approx 600g

juice of 1/2 **lemon**

1 tablespoon freshly chopped **dill**

beaten **egg** for glaze

Sauce

150ml **crème fraîche**

1/2 teaspoons **Dijon mustard**

salt and **pepper**

new potatoes

green veg

1 Preheat the oven to 180°C fan oven/200°C/gas 6. Grease a flat baking tray.

2 Put the flour, xanthan gum, butter and a pinch of salt in a bowl. Rub in the butter until you have breadcrumbs. Use a food processor if you have one. Add the egg and water and mix to a soft dough.

3 Gluten-free pastry is quite fragile, so lay a sheet of cling film on the work surface and sprinkle with flour. Roll out the pastry to about 1cm thick. Put the salmon on one half, squeeze over the lemon juice, sprinkle over the dill and season. Wet the edges of the pastry with water and fold over using the cling film. Cut off any excess and pinch the edges together.

4 Brush with beaten egg. Still using the cling film, carefully pull onto a greased, flat baking sheet. Remove the cling film by careful sliding it out from underneath. Bake in the oven for 40 minutes. The top should be golden brown.

5 Meanwhile, mix together the sauce ingredients and cook the potatoes and veg.

Sliced Pork Steaks with Honey & Coriander Sauce

Pork is now one of the more inexpensive meats to buy. Here, I have recommended buying 3 steaks to feed 4 people and it makes plenty.

1 1/2 mugs **basmati rice**

250g **mangetout**, halved

Sauce

20g **butter**, measure using packet

1 tablespoon freshly grated **ginger**

6 **spring onions**, chopped

grated zest of 1/2 an **orange**

juice of an **orange**

3 tablespoons **honey**

1 mug/300ml **water**

1 **GF chicken stock cube**

2 tablespoons **cornflour**

2 tablespoons freshly chopped **coriander**

1 tablespoon **olive oil**

4 **pork steaks**

1 Put the rice on to cook. Once the rice has cooked, add the mangetout to the pan. Put the lid back on the pan and remove from the heat.

2 Meanwhile, make the sauce. Heat the butter in a small pan and add the ginger and spring onions. Fry for one minute. Mix together the orange zest, juice, honey, water, stock cube and cornflour in a bowl. Add to the pan and bring to the boil; the sauce should thicken. Add the chopped coriander just before serving.

3 Heat the oil in a frying pan and add the steaks, fry for 2 minutes each side, seasoning well. Remove from the pan and cut into strips.

4 Stir the mangetout into the rice and serve with the pork on top. Drizzle over with the sauce.

Crunchy Oriental Cod with Lime & Honey Relish

This a great way to use polenta instead of needing to have, or make, gluten-free breadcrumbs. It provides that same delicious crunch.

400ml tin **coconut milk**

2 mugs/600ml **water**

1 1/2 mugs **basmati rice**

2 **pack choi**, thinly sliced

Chilli ginger relish

2 tablespoons toasted **sesame oil**

2 tablespoons freshly grated **ginger**

1 **fat red chilli**, chopped

6 **spring onions**, chopped

juice of a **lime**

2 tablespoons **honey**

4 **cod steaks**

1 beaten **egg**

1/4 mug **coarse polenta**

2 teaspoons **5 spice powder**

1 tablespoon **olive oil**

1 Put the coconut milk and water in a saucepan and bring to the boil. Add the rice and simmer, with a lid on the pan, for 12 minutes. Take off the heat and add the pak choi. Replace the lid and leave until needed.

2 Meanwhile, make the relish. Heat the oil in a small saucepan and add the ginger, chilli and onions. Fry for 1 minute.

3 Add the lime juice, honey and season. Bring to the boil and then take off the heat.

4 Cut the cod steaks into strips (see photo). Put the beaten egg in a bowl and mix the polenta and 5 spice on a plate. Dip the fish first in the egg and then in the polenta mix.

5 Heat the oil in a frying pan and fry the fish for 2 minutes on 2 sides until the outside is lightly browned.

6 Stir the pak choi into the rice. Serve the fish on top of the rice, with the relish over the top.

King Prawns with Coconut & Pak Choi Rice

Great dinner party food, especially if you love prawns. If you cook this in a good pan, wok, or hob to oven casserole, you can take it straight to the table as it looks so good.

4 tablespoons **sesame oil**

1 ½ mugs **basmati rice**

1 teaspoon **cumin seeds**

1 **cinnamon stick**

4 **lime leaves**

400ml tin **coconut milk**

2 mugs/600ml **water**

2 **pak choi**

3 cloves **garlic**, finely chopped

1 tablespoon freshly grated **ginger**

1 fat **red chilli**, finely chopped

250g **chestnut mushrooms**, sliced

500g raw **king prawns**

juice of a **lime**

2 tablespoons **GF Thai fish sauce**

1 tablespoon freshly chopped **coriander**

1 Heat 2 tablespoons of the sesame oil in a large frying pan or wok. Add the rice and cook until it absorbs the oil.

2 Add the cumin seeds, cinnamon stick, lime leaves, coconut milk and water. Season and bring to the boil. Simmer, with a lid on the pan, for 12 minutes.

3 Once the rice is cooked, thinly slice the pak choi and place on top of the rice. Cover with the pan lid and leave to stand.

4 Heat the other 2 tablespoons of sesame oil in a frying pan. Add the garlic, ginger and chilli and fry for 30 seconds.

5 Add the mushrooms and fry for 1 minute, stirring frequently to make sure the ginger does not burn.

6 Add the prawns and fry until they turn pink. Add the lime juice and the fish sauce. Cook until the sauce bubbles.

7 Pile on top of the rice and sprinkle over the coriander.

Cod with Tarragon Cream Sauce

It is best to use fresh tarragon to make the sauce, but you could use just one teaspoon of dried and simmer the sauce for 2 minutes. Tarragon is quite a hardy herb and will stay alive in the garden through the winter, and then begins to grow again in the spring, but you can still harvest a few sprigs.

5 medium **potatoes**, peeled and cut into 3cm chunks

1 large head of **broccoli**, stalks chopped, the rest cut into small pieces

25g **butter**, measure using packet

Sauce

25g **butter**, measure using packet

1 teaspoon **GF flour**

1 mug/300ml **single cream**

2 tablespoons freshly chopped **tarragon**

1 tablespoon **olive oil**

4 **cod steaks**

1   Put the potatoes and the chopped stalks from the broccoli in boiling water, and simmer for 7 minutes. Add the broccoli heads and simmer for a further 5 minutes. Drain and return to the pan. Add the butter, season well and mash together.

2   Meanwhile, make the sauce in a small saucepan. Heat the butter and add the flour, mix together and cook until it begins to bubble. Add the cream, tarragon and some salt and pepper. Bring to the boil, the sauce should thicken a little.

3   Heat the oil in a frying pan and add the cod steaks. Fry on each side for 2–3 minutes, longer if you have thicker steaks. The fish should be lightly browned and just cooked through.

Pork Steaks with Spinach & Apple Salad

You will need to keep an eye on the potatoes as they cook. Don't have the heat too high, or they may burn. This is an excellent way of getting quick roast potatoes. You could use them with all kinds of meals.

4 medium **potatoes**, cut into 2cm cubes

1 tablespoon **olive oil**

Dressing

juice of a **lemon**

2 tablespoons **olive oil**

1 tablespoon **honey**

1 teaspoon **wholegrain mustard**

salt and **pepper**

Salad

100g **fresh spinach**, roughly chopped

1/2 mug/50g **pine nuts**

1 **golden delicious apple**, cut into thin strips

1 tablespoon **olive oil**

4 **pork steaks**

1　Heat a tablespoon of oil in a medium-sized frying pan and add the potatoes, along with salt and pepper. Fry, with a lid on the pan, for 20 minutes. Keep turning the potatoes to get even browning.

2　Meanwhile, mix together the dressing ingredients. Mix the salad ingredients in a bowl and add the dressing just before serving.

3　Heat the other tablespoon of oil in a frying pan, fry the pork steaks for 2-3 minutes each side, depending on the thickness of the steaks. Season well as you cook.

4　Serve the steaks, potatoes and salad together.

Quick Coq au Vin

This classic French dish usually takes a few hours in the oven when it is made with chicken thighs. We have speeded things up here by using chicken breast and it is equally mouthwatering.

1 tablespoon **olive oil**

400g/10 **shallots**, halved

2 **carrots**, thinly sliced

3 **chicken breasts**, cut into large chunks

2 tablespoons **GF flour**

1 mug/300ml **water** + 1 tablespoon **GF liquid chicken stock**, or a **stock cube**

1 ½ mugs/½ bottle **red wine**

1 tablespoon **soft brown sugar**

2 **bay leaves**

250g **chestnut mushrooms**, sliced

6 medium **potatoes**, peeled and cut into 3cm chunks

50g **butter**, measure using packet

2 tablespoons **single or double cream**

sprouting broccoli

1 Heat the oil in a large saucepan or wok. Add the shallots and carrots and fry until they begin to brown.

2 Add the chicken and fry until it is no longer pink on the outside.

3 Add the flour and mix well. Add the water, stock, wine, sugar, bay leaves and mushrooms. Stir well and bring to the boil. The sauce should thicken slightly. Put a lid on the pan and turn down to simmer for 20 minutes.

4 Meanwhile, add the potatoes to a pan of boiling water. Simmer for 10-12 minutes or until tender. Drain and return to the pan. Mash with the butter and cream, season well. Put the lid on the pan to keep warm.

5 While the potatoes are cooking, cook the broccoli, drain and return to the pan.

6 Serve the Coq au Vin with the mash and broccoli.

Gluten-free does not mean we can't bake any more and can't have cakes and cookies! I loved developing these recipes. My family, who can eat wheat etc, actually prefer the non-gluten cakes and cookies.

TESTER #7

Hannah

The phrase 'busy young professional' would probably sum me up fairly well and I have been GF for just under two years. I suffered for years with pain, discomfort and daily nausea. The change has been incredible. I feel so much better and have lots more energy.

One recipe I tried was the 'Tortilla Layered Beef and Bean Pie' - great meal - easy to make, really tasty, and my first attempt even looked like the picture in the book!

I get stuck making lots of risottos and nothing else so I am looking for some new ideas for meals. I used to love baking, but stopped when I changed to a gluten-free diet as the recipes seemed too confusing or did not turn out well. I'm now inspired to get baking again.

Seeded Soda Bread

Soda bread is one of the easiest and quickest ways to make bread. It is best eaten the day it is made, but is also OK to freeze. If you freeze it in slices, you can get out just as much as you need.

1 ½ mugs/350g **GF white bread flour**

1 teaspoon **xanthan gum**

3 teaspoons **GF bicarbonate of soda**

2 teaspoons **GF cream of tartar**

1 teaspoon **salt**

2 tablespoons **soft brown sugar**

2 tablespoons **pumpkin seeds**

1 tablespoon **sesame seeds**

1 tablespoon **sunflower seeds**

1 mug/300ml **buttermilk**

⅓ mug/100ml **water**

1 beaten **egg** to brush the top

1 Preheat the oven to 200°C fan oven/220°C/gas 7. Grease a baking tray.

2 Put all the dry ingredients in a large bowl and mix together.

3 Mix in the liquids and it should form a soft dough. Turn out onto a floured surface and knead gently to ensure everything is well mixed. Form into a round and place on the baking tray.

4 Brush the top with beaten egg and then make slashes across the top of the loaf.

5 Bake in the oven for 45-50 minutes. The top should be lovely and brown. The loaf should sound hollow when tapped on the bottom.

TESTER #8

I am not gluten-intolerant, but, following advice from Gavin, my trainer, I have been eating wheat-free for the last 2 years and have lost 7 inches around my stomach.
I missed bread and so have loved these GF breads. I have definitely enjoyed being a taste-tester over the last year or so whilst we have been writing this book!

Ron

Brown Seeded Loaf

I tried many variations before deciding on this recipe. The recipes on the bread flour packets tend to turn out somewhat solid. The crust on this loaf is absolutely lovely. This recipe needs to be measured quite accurately, so my usual mug measures unfortunately have to be dispensed with on this occasion.

125ml **warm water**

2 tablespoons **sugar**

4 teaspoons **dried yeast**

1 tablespoon **cider** or **white wine vinegar**

2 **eggs** + 2 **egg whites**

80ml **olive oil**

150ml **warm water**

3 tablespoons **honey**

1 tablespoon **black treacle**

80ml **apple juice**

500g **GF brown bread flour**

2 teaspoons **xanthan gum**

1 teaspoon **salt**

2 tablespoons **pumpkin seeds**

1 tablespoon **sesame seeds**

1 tablespoon **sunflower seeds**

1 Put 125ml warm water and sugar in a 500ml jug (leaves room for the yeast to work). Sprinkle the yeast over the water and stir until it has dissolved. Leave for 5-10 minutes until the yeast has a good foam over the top.

2 Mix together the vinegar, eggs and egg whites, oil, 250ml water, honey, black treacle and apple juice.

3 Mix the flour, xanthan gum, salt and seeds in a large bowl (I used a food mixer). Add the egg mixture and the yeast mixture and mix until everything is combined. You should have more of a batter than a dough. Turn out into a loaf tin until it is 3/4 full. If you have extra dough, form it into small bread buns and cook for about 30 minutes at the end.

4 Leave in a good warm place for about 1 hour. The dough should double in size.

5 Place in a preheated oven at 170°C fan oven/190°C/gas 5 for 70 minutes. Take out of the tin and place on a tray and bake for a further 15 minutes. The loaf should have a 'hollow' sound when tapped on its bottom.

White Bread Loaf

This needs to be measured quite accurately, so my usual mug measures have to be dispensed with. Freeze in slices so you can get a few out at a time.

125ml **warm water**

2 tablespoons **sugar**

4 teaspoons **dried yeast**

1 tablespoon **cider** or **white wine vinegar**

2 **eggs** + 2 **egg** whites

80ml **olive oil**

150ml **warm water**

3 tablespoons **honey**

80ml **apple juice**

500g **white, GF bread flour**

2 teaspoons **xanthan gum**

1 teaspoon **salt**

1 Put the 125ml water and sugar in a 500ml jug (leaves room for the yeast to work). Sprinkle the yeast over the water and stir until it has dissolved. Leave for 5-10 minutes, until the yeast has a good foam over the top.

2 Mix together the vinegar, eggs and egg whites, oil, 250ml water, honey and apple juice.

3 Mix the flour, xanthan gum and salt in a large bowl (I used a food mixer). Add the egg mixture and the yeast mixture and mix until everything is combined. You should have more of a batter than a dough. Turn out into a loaf tin.

4 Leave in a good warm place for about 1 hour. The dough should double in size.

5 Place in a preheated oven at 170°C fan oven/190°C/gas 5 for 65 minutes. The loaf should have a 'hollow' sound when tapped on its bottom. If it doesn't, take it out of the tin and place it back in the oven for another 5-10 minutes.

£0.42 /PERSON — SERVES 12 — EASE ★★★★☆ — PREP 15 MINS — COOK 25 MINS — COOLING 1 HOUR — V

Chocolate Cake with Chocolate Ganache

If you ever thought that eating gluten-free was the end to yummy, gooey, oozy, naughty, sticky chocolate cake that melted in your mouth, you were wrong!

230g softened **butter**, measure using packet

1 1/4 mugs/230g **caster sugar**

4 **eggs**

1 1/2 mugs/230g **rice flour**

1 1/2 teaspoons **GF baking powder**

1 teaspoon **vanilla extract**

1 tablespoon **cocoa**

1 1/2 tablespoons **milk**

250ml/almost 1 mug **double cream**

250g **milk chocolate**

1 Preheat the oven to 180°C fan oven/200°C/gas 7. Grease and line the bottom of 2 x 19cm cake tins.

2 Beat the butter and sugar together until light and fluffy.

3 Add the eggs, one at a time, beating well between each.

4 Add the flour, baking powder, vanilla extract, cocoa and milk. Fold in gently until smoothly mixed.

5 Spoon into the 2 tins and spread out evenly.

6 Place in the oven for 20–25 minutes until they bounce back a little when gently pressed. Take out of the oven and cool.

7 To make the ganache, heat the cream until it just boils. Take off the heat and add the chocolate, stirring until it melts.

8 Leave in the fridge for about 1 hour, the ganache should thicken.

9 Sandwich the 2 cakes together with the ganache and spread the rest on top.

Maple Syrup Soaked Almond & Citrus Cake

Surprisingly light in texture with a gorgeous spiced citrus tang. It is special enough to use as a dessert with some crème fraîche.

300g **ground almonds**

250g **light brown sugar**

2 teaspoons **GF baking powder**

5 **eggs**

200ml **vegetable oil**

2 teaspoons **maple syrup**

grated zest of a **lemon** and an **orange**

Syrup

juice of an **orange** and a **lemon**

5 tablespoons **maple syrup**

3 **cloves**

1 **cinnamon stick**

yoghurt to serve

1 Preheat the oven to 160°C fan oven/180°C/gas 5. Grease and line the bottom of a 23cm springform tin.

2 Mix together the dry ingredients for the cake.

3 Whisk together the eggs, oil, maple syrup and orange and lemon zest. Add to the dry ingredients and mix well. Pour into the tin.

4 Put in the oven for 45-50 minutes. The cake should be lightly browned and not wobbly when shaken.

5 Put the syrup ingredients into a small pan and bring to the boil. Simmer gently for 5 minutes; the syrup ingredients should thicken.

6 When the cake has cooled slightly, loosen the sides of the cake tin and spoon the syrup over the top.

7 Serve with a blob of yoghurt.

Lemon Drizzle Cake

Gorgeous, lemon drizzle. I have always put plenty of sugar on the top of this cake, but Tim encouraged me to add more - it worked! It is a must to master for us gluten-freers.

225g softened **butter**, measure using packet

1 mug/225g **caster sugar**

4 **eggs**

1 1/3 mugs/275g **GF self-raising flour**

1 teaspoon **GF baking powder**

1 teaspoon **xanthan gum**

4 tablespoons **milk**

zest of 2 **large lemons**

Topping

3/4 mug/175g **granulated sugar**

juice of 2 **lemons**

1 Preheat the oven to 160°C fan oven/180°C/gas 4. Grease and line a 30 x 23cm traybake tin.

2 In a mixing bowl, cream together the butter and sugar.

3 Add the eggs, one at a time, beating well in between.

4 Add the rest of the cake ingredients. Fold in until evenly mixed.

5 Pour into the traybake and spread out evenly. Put in the oven for 35–40 minutes. The cake should spring back when pressed gently.

6 Leave to cool slightly. Mix together the topping and spread over the top of the cake.

TESTER #9

Graham & Anne

I (Anne) have always enjoyed cooking and baking for my family and friends in the past. Since having to cut gluten out of my diet, cooking became a chore and eating generally much less enjoyable. In Joy's book I found the recipes delicious and interesting, with the cakes and pastries exceptional. So much so, they would not be out of place in the Ritz Tea-room! This book excites me and makes me want to get cooking again!

I (Graham) am not gluten-free but thought "wow I want to try these!". Now everyone can enjoy the same meal.

Date & Walnut Slice

OK, so a date and walnut slice may not sound like the height of gastronomic advancement. It's not, but it ain't half tasty!

250g chopped **dates**

just under a mug/250g **boiling water**

75g **butter**, measure using packet

1 mug/180g **dark, soft brown** sugar

1 ½ mugs/275g **GF self-raising flour**

½ mug/50g chopped **walnuts**

1 **egg**, beaten

1 Preheat the oven to 160°C fan oven/180°C/gas 6. Grease and line a 23x30cm traybake tin.

2 Put the chopped dates and the butter in the boiling water and leave to stand for 5 minutes.

3 Meanwhile, mix together the sugar, flour and walnuts in a bowl.

4 Add the egg to the date mixture and then pour into the dry ingredients. Gently mix together. Pour into the traybake tin and spread out evenly.

5 Bake in the oven for 40 minutes. The cake should spring back slightly when gently pressed.

Zesty Lime & Coconut Cakes

Ben thought it would be fun to decorate these cakes. Clearly he was frustrated at being confined to straight lines, so decided to make his protest clear!

175g **softened butter**, measure using packet

3/4 mug/175g **caster sugar**

3 **eggs**

3/4 mug/125g **rice flour**

2 teaspoons **GF baking powder**

1 teaspoon **xanthan gum**

1/2 mug/50g **desiccated coconut**

juice and rind of 4 **limes**

Icing

1 mug **icing sugar**

juice of a **lime**

1   Preheat the oven to 160°C fan oven/180°C/ gas 4. Put 16 cake cases on trays.

2   Cream the butter and sugar together. Add the eggs, one at a time, and beating well between each addition.

3   Sift together the rice flour, baking powder and xanthan gum. Add to the bowl, along with the coconut and the lime zest, and juice and fold in gently.

4   Spoon the mixture into the cases. Bake in the oven for 25 minutes. The cakes should spring back a little when pressed.

5   Put the icing sugar in a bowl and add enough lime juice to make a stiff paste. Once the cakes are cooled, drizzle over the tops. Leave to set.

Double Chocolate Chip Muffins

We have a resident 'chocoholic' in the kitchen and the office, so we had to make these. If you need another excuse to make these, try the recipe on page 210 for Cherry & Chocolate Muffin Sundaes.

1 ½ mugs/300g **GF self-raising flour**. Take out 2 tablespoons of the flour and replace with 2 tablespoons of **cocoa**

1 teaspoon **GF baking powder**

1 teaspoon **xanthan gum**

2/3 mug/175g **caster sugar**

100g packet **chocolate chips**

2 **eggs**

100g melted **butter**, measure using packet

2/3 mug/200ml **milk**

1 Preheat the oven to 180°C fan oven/200°C/gas 6. Prepare 18 muffin cases in tins.

2 Put the dry ingredients in a large bowl.

3 Mix together the wet ingredients in a large jug and add to the bowl. Mix well, but do not beat.

4 Spoon into the muffin cases. Makes 24 using small cases, or 18 if using large.

5 Bake in the oven for 25 minutes. The muffins should spring back when gently pressed. If you use smaller cake cases, you will only need to cook them for about 20 minutes.

Carrot Cake Traybake

If you have a food processor, cut the carrots into pieces, place in the processor and blitz until they resemble breadcrumbs. Add the raisins and nuts and pulse a few times. This saves a lot of chopping and gives the perfect texture.

4 **eggs**

1 ¼ mugs/215g **dark brown sugar**

2/3 mug/165ml **sunflower oil**

2 mugs/360g **GF self-raising flour**

1 teaspoon **xanthan gum**

4 **medium carrots**, finely grated

zest and juice of an **orange**

2/3 mug/100g **raisins**, chopped

3/4 mug/100g **pecan nuts**, chopped

1/3 mug/25g **desiccated coconut**

Topping

300g **Philadelphia cheese**

5 tablespoons **maple syrup**

50g chopped **pecans** to decorate

1 Preheat the oven to 160°C fan oven/180°C/gas 4. Grease and line a 20 x 30cm traybake tin.

2 Put the egg yolks in a bowl and add the sugar. Beat until light and paler in colour.

3 Gradually add the oil, beating well as you do.

4 Add the flour, xanthan gum, carrots, orange, raisins, nuts and coconut. Mix well, but don't beat.

5 Whisk the egg whites until they form soft peaks. Put half into the mixture and gently fold in. This will loosen the mixture a little. Fold in the other half of the eggs, being careful not to lose the air you have put in.

6 Pour into the traybake tin and level out. Place in the oven for 35–40 minutes. The top of the cake should bounce back a little when pressed lightly.

7 Once the cake is cooled, mix the topping ingredients together and spread over evenly. Cut into squares and keep in a cake tin if it lasts long enough!

Cranberry & Cream Cheese Muffins with a Hint of Ginger

The blob of cream cheese in the centre of these muffins makes them quite unusual. The tanginess of the cranberries makes a good fusion.

100g **Philadelphia cheese**

2 tablespoons **sugar**

1 mug/150g **cranberries**

3 pieces **crystallised ginger**, chopped

2 mugs/400g **GF self-raising flour**

1 teaspoon **GF baking powder**

2/3 mug/160g **granulated sugar**

2 large **eggs**

1/2 mug/150ml **sunflower oil**

2/3 mug/200ml **milk**

1 Mix together the Philadelphia and one tablespoon of the sugar in a small bowl. Set to one side.

2 Put the cranberries, one tablespoon of sugar, ginger and a tablespoon water in a small pan and heat until the cranberries soften a little. Remove from the heat and leave to cool.

3 Preheat the oven to 180°C fan oven/200°C/gas 6. Prepare 18 bun cases.

4 In a large bowl, mix together the sugar, flour, baking powder. Add the cranberry mixture and mix well.

5 In a separate bowl, beat the eggs, oil and milk together and stir into the dry ingredients. Spoon into the bun cases.

6 Make a little hollow in each one and add a blob of cream cheese, about one teaspoon.

7 Bake in the oven for 25 minutes. They should be nicely browned and spring back a little when pressed.

Classic Victoria Sandwich

250g **butter**, softened

1 mug/250g **caster sugar**

4 **eggs**

1 teaspoon **vanilla extract**

1 1/2 tablespoons **milk**

1 1/3 mugs/250g **rice flour**

1 teaspoon **GF baking powder**

2 tablespoons **good quality raspberry jam**

1 mug/300ml **double cream**

icing sugar to dredge over the top

1 Preheat the oven to 180°C fan oven/200°C/gas 6. Grease and line 2 x 20cm cake tins.

2 In a bowl or food mixer, beat the butter and sugar together until light and fluffy.

3 Add the eggs, one at a time, and beat well between each addition.

4 Add the vanilla, milk, rice flour and baking powder and gently fold in. Take care not to over mix, as the rice flour can become a little 'gluey'.

5 Bake in the oven for 20 minutes. Leave to cool, out of the tin, on a cooling tray.

6 Once cooled, spread the bottom cake with the raspberry jam. Beat the cream and spread over the jam. Top with the other cake and sift some icing sugar over.

£0.29 /PIECE · MAKES 18 · EASE ★★☆☆☆ · PREP 15 MINS · COOK 30 MINS · V

Gooey Hazelnut Brownies

Love brownies and have missed them since you started eating gluten-free...?

200g **dark chocolate**

125g **butter**, measure using packet

1 mug/210g **soft brown sugar**

1/2 mug/100g **GF self-raising flour**

1 tablespoon **cocoa**

1 teaspoon **xanthan gum**

1 teaspoon **GF baking powder**

100g packet chopped **hazelnuts**

3 large **eggs**, beaten

1 Preheat the oven to 160°C fan oven/180°C/gas 6. Grease and line a 30 x 20cm traybake tin.

2 Melt the chocolate and butter in a bowl over a pan of simmering water. Leave to cool for a few minutes.

3 Mix the dry ingredients together in a bowl.

4 Add the beaten eggs and mix well.

5 Add the cooled chocolate and butter and mix well.

6 Pour into the tin and bake in the oven for 30 minutes. The top will form a crust, but the insides should be quite gooey.

7 You can scatter a few more chopped hazelnuts over the top if you wish.

Christina

TESTER #10

I am a wife, mother of two and we have been gluten-free for 5 years. Both my husband and my daughter were diagnosed with coeliac disease. This means we eat at home a lot.

The 'Gooey Hazelnut Brownies' are excellent! Best GF brownies I have made that did not involve ground almonds. I like those kind too, but sometimes it is nice to just have brownies!

Orange & Lemon Polenta Cake

To decorate the top, peel the orange with a sharp knife to get rid of any pith. Cut into thin slices and halve.

200g softened **butter**, measure using packet

¾ mug/200g **caster sugar**

3 **eggs**

1 ½ mugs/180g **ground almonds**

¾ mug/120g **fine polenta**

1 ½ teaspoons **GF baking powder**

zest of an **orange** and a **lemon**

Topping

juice of an **orange** and **lemon**

4 tablespoons **granulated sugar**

lemon curd for filling

1 **orange** to decorate (optional)

1 Preheat the oven to 160°C fan oven/180°C/ gas 5. Grease and line 2 x 18cm cake tins.

2 Beat together the butter and sugar. Add the eggs one at a time, beating in as you go.

3 Add the rest of the cake ingredients and gently fold in.

4 Divide between the cake tins and smooth out. Place in the oven for 35 minutes.

5 Leave to cool. Sandwich the cakes together with the lemon curd. Mix the juices and sugar together and carefully spread over the top of the cake.

£0.22 /PERSON | SERVES 24 | EASE ★★☆☆☆ | PREP 25 MINS | COOK 25 MINS | V

Breakfast Munchies
with Pumpkin Seeds & Cranberries

These make a good alternative to the expensive 'goody bars' you can buy ready-made and they are about half the price. Again, be careful with the oats if you are coeliac, as 'normal' ones can contain traces of wheat. See page 8 for completely gluten-free oats. Also some rice krispies contain barley, so if you are coeliac then check the packet.

397g tin **condensed milk**

50g **butter**, measure using packet

2/3 mug/100g **raisins**

2/3 mug/100g **cranberries**

1/4 mug/50g **mixed peel**

50g **flaked almonds**

1 mug/70g **GF rice krispies**

2 mugs/200g **GF rolled oats**

1/4 mug/30g **sunflower seeds**

1/4 mug/30g **pumpkin seeds**

1 Preheat the oven to 160°C fan oven/180°C/gas 5. Line a 20 x 30cm traybake tin.

2 Put the condensed milk and butter in a small pan and gently bring to the boil.

3 Mix the dry ingredients together in a large bowl. Add the condensed milk and mix well.

4 Press into the tin and bake in the oven for 25 minutes.

Fat Rascals

Fat Rascals originated in Yorkshire in the 1880's. They have lately been made more famous, as they were included in the menu of Betty's Tea Shop in Harrogate. If you have never visited this establishment, it has to go on your bucket list.

1 ³/₄/320g mug **GF self-raising flour**

175g **butter**, measure using packet

¹/₂ mug/115g **caster sugar**

¹/₂ mug/75g **sultanas**

zest of an **orange**

1 tablespoon **mixed peel**

¹/₃ mug 75g **glacé cherries**, roughly chopped

¹/₂ mug/50g **toasted flaked almonds**

¹/₄ mug/50ml **milk**

1 beaten **egg**

1 beaten **egg** to brush

1 Preheat the oven to 180°C fan oven/200°C/gas 6. Grease 2 baking sheets.

2 Put the flour, butter and sugar in the food processor and whizz until you have something resembling breadcrumbs.

3 Tip into a large bowl and add the sultanas, orange zest, mixed peel, cherries and almonds. Mix together.

4 Add one of the eggs with the milk and add to the bowl. Mix together to form a soft dough.

5 Turn out onto a floured surface and press down until the dough is 1.5cm thick. Cut 6cm rounds and place on a baking sheet. Brush with the remaining beaten egg.

6 Bake in the oven for 15–20 minutes. The tops should be nicely browned.

Banana & Chocolate Chip Cookies

How do you get bananas into a cookie? Easy, get somebody to dry them for you first.

125g softened **butter**, measure using packet

1 mug/180g **soft brown sugar**

1 **egg**

1 teaspoon **vanilla extract**

100g **milk chocolate chips**

1 mug/200g **GF self-raising flour**

3/4 mug/75g **GF rolled oats**

1/3 mug/50g **banana chips**, crushed

+ 1/4/30g **banana chips** to decorate

1 Preheat the oven to 180°C fan oven/200°C/gas 6. Grease 2 large baking trays.

2 Beat together the butter and sugar. Add the egg and vanilla extract and beat well.

3 Add the chocolate chips, flour, rolled oats and crushed banana chips. Mix well.

4 Tip the mixture onto a surface and divide into 24 pieces. Roll each one into a ball and then place on the tray and squash down slightly. Press a banana chip into the top of each cookie.

5 Bake in the oven for 12 minutes. The cookies should be lightly browned, but will still be a little squidgy in the middle.

🌐 Have you made polenta cookies yet? If not, why not start here: www.noshbooks.com/polenta-cookie

Sweet Scones

If you don't have a food processor, rub the butter into the flour with your fingertips. Add the liquid and mix together. If you want cheese scones, omit the sugar and add 3/4 mug grated Cheddar cheese.

140g **butter**, measure using packet

2 mugs/400g **GF self-raising flour**

1 teaspoon **xanthan gum**

1/3 mug/60g **sugar**

1 **egg**, beaten in a mug + enough **milk** to make 3/4 mug in total

1 beaten **egg** to brush the tops

Serve with **jam** and **cream**

1 Preheat the oven to 180°C fan oven/200°C/gas 6. Grease a baking tray.

2 Put the butter, flour and xanthan gum in a food processor and blitz until the mixture resembles breadcrumbs.

3 Add the sugar, milk and egg and pulse the processor a few times until the mixture comes together.

4 Tip out onto a floured surface and squash into a round shape. Handle as little as possible. Cut into 6cm rounds. Place on the baking tray and brush with beaten egg.

5 Place in the oven for 20 minutes. The tops should be golden brown.

Hazelnut Delights

These cookies almost have a shortbread taste. I love the addition of nuts to cookies. Unfortunately, it means I tend to eat rather more than I should.

130g **butter**, measure using packet

1/2 mug/115g **caster sugar**

1 **egg**

1 1/4 mugs/225g **GF self-raising flour**

1 teaspoon **vanilla extract**

1/2 mug/50g **ground hazelnuts**

1 Preheat the oven to 180°C fan oven/200°C/gas 6. Grease 2 flat baking trays.

2 Cream together the butter and sugar in a bowl or food mixer. Add the egg and beat well.

3 Add the flour and vanilla extract. Mix together to form a soft dough.

4 Put the hazelnuts in a small bowl. Tip the cookie dough out onto a floured surface and cut into 24 pieces. Roll each one into a ball and then roll in the ground hazelnuts, pressing as much as you can into the surface of the cookie.

5 Place on the baking trays and press down lightly, no need to flatten. Bake in the oven for 12 minutes. The cookies should be lovely and golden.

£ 0.15 /EACH · SERVES 24 · EASE ★★☆☆☆ · PREP 15 MINS · COOK 20 MINS · OK TO FREEZE · V

Orange & Cranberry Cookies with Orange Frosting

If you don't have a piping bag for the decoration, just drizzle from a spoon and tell people you were going for a rustic look!

170g softened **butter**, measure using packet

just under a mug/175g **light brown sugar**

2 **eggs**

1 teaspoon **vanilla extract**

1 1/2 mugs/165g **GF oats**

3/4 mug/160g **GF self-raising flour**

3/4 mug/100g **dried cranberries**

zest of an **orange**

Icing

1 mug/185g **icing sugar**

2 tablespoons fresh **orange juice**

1 Preheat the oven to 180°C fan oven/200°C/gas 6. Grease 2 flat baking trays.

2 Beat the butter and sugar together in a mixing bowl or food mixer. Add the eggs, one at a time, and beat well.

3 Add the rest of the cookie ingredients and mix to a soft dough.

4 Put dessertspoons of the mixture on the trays, leaving them 5 cm apart so they have room to spread.

5 Bake in the oven for 20 minutes.

6 Leave to cool. Mix together the icing sugar and enough orange juice to make a 'dribbleable' icing. Put the icing in a piping bag and drizzle over the cookies.

🌐 See more cookie recipes online:
www.noshbooks.com/gf-cookies

Almond Macaroons
Just How I Remember Them

These look like the macaroons I knew as I grew up. I loved them then and I love them now.

4 medium **egg** whites
½ mug/125g **caster sugar**
1 mug/125g **ground almonds**
¼ teaspoon **almond extract**
flaked almonds to decorate

1 Preheat the oven to 160°C fan oven/180°C/gas 5. Line 2 flat trays with greaseproof paper.

2 Whisk the egg whites until they are stiff. Gently stir in the sugar, then the almonds and the almond extract.

3 Take dessertspoonfuls of the mixture and place on the trays. Put the almonds on top.

4 Place in the oven for 15 minutes. The tops should be lightly browned.

5 Leave on the trays to cool.

Cherry & Chocolate Muffin Sundaes

Yes, there is a whole muffin in the centre of these sundaes! But you can layer them however you like.

Chocolate sauce

4 tablespoons **double cream**

25g **butter**, measure using packet

4 tablespoons **soft brown sugar**

100g **dark chocolate**

370g packet good quality **cherry pie filling**

vanilla ice cream

8 **GF double chocolate muffins** (you can make them, see page 184 or buy them)

1 mug/300ml **double cream**, lightly whipped

1   Make the muffins, see page 184.

2   To make the chocolate sauce, put all the ingredients in a small pan and gently heat. Bring to the boil and allow to bubble for 30 seconds. Leave to cool slightly.

3   Make up the sundaes by layering the ingredients (see photo). We put a whole muffin in here and then crumbled the other two.

🌍 Did someone say trifle? Here's one:
www.noshbooks.com/trifle

Baileys & Banana Cake Sundaes with Caramel Sauce

This is a great way to use up the Baileys after Christmas, or an excuse to buy some more! Baileys will contain traces of malt, so if you are coeliac, or very sensitive to gluten, you may need to give this one a miss. I found it OK, as the amount of Baileys per portion is quite small.

You can buy a gluten-free banana cake from Sainsburys if you don't want to make it.

Banana Cake

70g **butter**, measure using packet

2/3 mug/125g soft **brown sugar**

1 **egg**

1 squashed **banana**

3/4 mug/140g **GF self-raising flour**

1 teaspoon **xanthan gum**

Caramel Sauce

50g **butter**, measure using packet

2 tablespoons **soft brown sugar**

4 tablespoons **double cream**

250g **mascarpone cream**

400ml **double cream**

500ml **GF vanilla custard**

3 **bananas**, sliced

1/2 mug **Baileys**

1/2 mug chopped **pecans**

1 To make the cake, preheat the oven to 160°C fan oven/180°C/gas 5 and grease a 20cm cake tin.

2 Beat together the butter and sugar. Add the egg and beat well. Add the squashed banana and beat well. Fold in the flour and xanthan gum.

3 Pour into the cake tin and bake in the oven for 30 minutes. Once cooked, remove from the tin, leave to cool and then break into chunks.

4 Make the caramel sauce by gently melting all the ingredients in a small saucepan, stirring continually and simmering for 1 minute.

5 Gently mix together the mascarpone and the cream.

6 Put the cake in the bottom of the sundae dishes, along with the bananas, and drizzle over the Baileys. Top with the caramel sauce, custard and cream. Sprinkle the nuts on top. You may not need to use all the cake.

Pancakes with Sticky Cinnamon Bananas

The reason I have specified White Flora or Trex in this and other pancake recipes is because it can be heated to a much higher temperature compared to normal oils, without burning. It also works well if you want to replace the bananas with fresh pineapple.

Pancakes

2/3 mug/130g **GF self-raising flour**

2 **eggs**

2/3 mug/200ml **milk**

White Flora to fry

Bananas

50g **butter**, measure using packet

4 **bananas,** thickly sliced

1 teaspoon **ground cinnamon**

2 tablespoons **runny honey**

1 Beat together the flour, egg and milk to make the pancake mixture.

2 Heat a small frying pan and add a small piece of White Flora or Trex. Pour 1/4 of the mixture into the heated pan. Cook the first side until the mixture starts to bubble and the underneath is nicely browned. Turn over and cook the reverse side. Repeat until all the mixture is used. Keep the pancakes in a warm place.

3 Heat the butter in a large frying pan and fry the bananas until they begin to brown. Add the honey and sprinkle the cinnamon over the bananas. Take off the heat. The heat from the pan will warm the honey.

4 Serve the bananas with the pancakes. Some yoghurt would go very nicely with them.

£ 0.41 /PERSON · SERVES 8 · EASE ★★★☆☆ · PREP 20 MINS · COOK 20 MINS · OK TO FREEZE ❄ · V

Really Rather Splendid Chocolate Roulade

We had a little bit of fun with this photo by first dredging with icing sugar and then with cocoa. Tim then scraped some shavings from a block of chocolate.

Roulade

175g **dark chocolate**

5 **eggs**, separated, keep both white and yoke

²/₃ mug/175g **caster sugar**

3 tablespoons **hot water**

Filling

1 mug/300ml **double cream**

Decoration

icing sugar

cocoa

45g bar of **chocolate**

1 Preheat the oven to 160°C fan oven/180°C/gas 5. Line a swiss roll tin with greaseproof paper and then lightly oil the paper.

2 Melt the chocolate in a bowl over a pan of simmering water.

3 Beat together the egg yolks and sugar until they are pale in colour and light and fluffy.

4 Add the hot water to the melted chocolate and pour it into the eggs and gently mix.

5 Beat the egg whites with clean beaters until they form stiff peaks. Gently fold into the chocolate mixture. Pour into the swiss roll tin and gently spread out.

6 Bake in the oven for 20 minutes.

7 Prepare a sheet of greaseproof paper on a work surface and sprinkle about 2 tablespoons of caster sugar over it. Once the cake is cooked, gently turn out onto the paper, leaving the original greaseproof on. Cover with a damp tea towel and leave until it is completely cool.

8 Remove the tea towel and the original greaseproof paper. Beat the cream until it forms soft peaks and then spread over the cake evenly. Use the greaseproof paper underneath to grip the cake and roll up the roulade. Dredge the top with a little icing sugar, cocoa and grated chocolate.

"Snickers" Sundaes

Gluten-free chocolate digestives are available on the internet, or you can buy "Trufree Chocolate Nobbles" in Waitrose. There is not a Snickers bar in sight, but it does taste like Snickers.

This was inspired by some ice cream Tim had on his honeymoon in Italy. He was very pleased that I managed to recreate the taste. He absolutely loves this recipe.

Chocolate Sauce

50g **butter**, measure using packet

100g **milk chocolate**

2 tablespoons **light brown sugar**

4 tablespoons **double cream**

Caramel sauce

50g **butter**, measure using packet

2 tablespoons **light brown sugar**

4 tablespoons **double cream**

2 tablespoons **peanut butter**

500ml tub **ice cream**

4 **GF chocolate digestives**, broken up

100g chopped **macadamian nuts**

1 To make the chocolate sauce, put all the ingredients in a pan and gently heat. Simmer for 30 seconds, stirring well. Set to one side until needed.

2 To make the caramel sauce, gently heat the butter, sugar and cream. Simmer for 2 minutes, making sure the sugar is dissolved. Stir in the peanut butter. Set to one side.

3 Layer the ice cream, sauces, nuts and biscuits to make a really naughty sundae.

Pear & Raspberry Coconut Crumble

I had never thought a crumble without flour and sugar could work, but this coconut crumble is absolutely lovely. You can vary the fruits; peaches work well, for example.

1kg **jar of pears** (Natures Best work well)

200g fresh **raspberries**

2 tablespoons **soft brown sugar**

Crumble top

1 1/2 mugs/110g **desiccated coconut**

2/3 mug/150g **caster sugar**

2 **egg whites**

1 Preheat the oven to 150°C fan oven/170°C/gas 4.

2 Drain the pears, then put them and the raspberries in a small casserole dish and sprinkle the brown sugar over.

3 Mix together the ingredients for the crumble topping in a bowl. Spread over the top of the fruit.

4 Place in the oven for 25 minutes. The top should be browned and crunchy.

index